She Found it at the Movies

WHAT THE CRITICS SAY...

'For anyone who thinks "sexy feminism" is an oxymoron, this collection will lay that hoary assumption to rest. The different entries by a wildly diverse group of women positively shimmer with hormonal palpitations and startle with acute judgments.'

Molly Haskell (Film critic, author: "From Reverence to Rape: the Treatment of Women in the Movies")

'Gives film criticism the vitamin-boost it needed, a female gaze bringing eroticism, sensuality and a new subversive intimacy to the critical act; the book celebrates not just desire but pleasure. Each of these essays is a seduction, leading you astray to the great seduction of the movies themselves.'

Peter Bradshaw (Film critic, The Guardian)

'A lush, incisive essay collection that brings together a diverse group of voices; an empathetic and potent take on female desire. For anyone interested in the ways women look at the world, these essays offer the female gaze in her most playful and intellectually curious form. The essays probe the multi-faceted nature of female desire, revealing the ways it intersects with race, gender identity, and age—they are celebratory and wrenching in equal measure. It's a timely exploration about women's passions: how they're formed, how they're felt, how they're curtailed. Readers will not only find themselves in these pages but be challenged to consider female desire in more complex ways.'

Angelica Jade Bastién (Vulture)

'Collapses the space between screen and body and foregrounds the reality of our very complex and always present bodies. While that space has long been dominated by so-called objectivity and clinical analysis, this collection dives into uncharted waters to explore, creating space for discussing desire instead of repressing it.'

Kiva Reardon (Toronto International Film Festival)

'At its best, a book of fiercely original writing and thinking, not only about cinema, but about ourselves.'

Mark Cousins (Writer and filmmaker, "The Story of Film")

'Celebrates women writers basking in the joy and power of films—to feel them as much as see them. It is jolting reminder that if you see a certain film at a certain time in your life, it can change your worldview.'

Cari Beauchamp (Film historian, author: "Without Lying Down" and "My First Time in Hollywood")

'Part confessional, part soapbox—this collection shares and glories in the secret heat of women's cinematic gaze. These tales of sexual awakenings and reorientations explore the appeal of stars as varied as Steve McQueen, Julie Andrews, Jada Pinkett-Smith and Timothée Chalamet—and assert the agency of the female and nonbinary viewer, the person who is supposed to be looked at, rather than looking. In an era when women's voices and roles in movie making are still squeezed into the margins, this chorus is more than welcome, it's essential.'

Joanna Scutts (Literary critic, social historian, author: "The Extra Woman")

'Rich, energising, teeming with theory, wit and feeling on a subject both essential and under-explored in film studies: how female viewers' desire is sparked and nourished by a cinema that rarely shares their gaze. A diverse, beautifully integrated ensemble of female critical voices, each one probing the project's core theme from a slightly different angle, covering youthful screen crushes and more mature reckonings with the conflict between cinematic and real-life sexuality. To read this book is to feel intense, intimate recognition of shared swoons, and also to see cinema and its icons through another's eyes: you'll emerge from this wildly entertaining, tactile enquiry with renewed appreciation for the ways in which the camera makes us look, and occasionally winks back at us.'

Guy Lodge (Film critic, Variety)

She Found it at the Movies

WOMEN WRITERS ON SEX, DESIRE AND CINEMA

EDITED BY CHRISTINA NEWLAND

Edited by Christina Newland
Cover design Katherine Knotts and Charles Newland
Printed in England by TJ International (Cornwall)

Published by Red Press
ISBN 978 1 912157 181 (Paperback)
ISBN 978 1 912157 198 (Ebook)

A catalogue record for this book is available from the British Library

Red Press Registered Offices:
6 Courtenay Close, Wareham, Dorset, BH20 4ED, England

www.redpress.co.uk
@redpresspub

#MyFemaleDesire

The deeper root of the word 'desire' links it to 'star' and 'shine'—as if our desires were the bright centres of our beings.

–J.D. McClatchy

CONTENTS

INNOCENCE AND EXPERIENCE

FANTASY AND DANGER

OUR BODIES, OUR SELVES

THE FEMALE GAZE

THOSE BLUE-EYED BOYS
Christina Newland

'Cinema is the ultimate pervert art. It doesn't give you what you desire—it tells you how to desire.'

–Slavoj Žižek

MY SORDID AFFAIR WITH movies began because I fell in love with a dead movie star. To my 13-year-old self, all the colour, romance and tragedy of classical Hollywood rested on the skinny shoulders of a young man with movie-blue eyes and a red windbreaker, who spoke in staccato poetry and shuffled his feet and whose slouch couldn't conceal his outrageous beauty. And by only 24 years old, an age that seemed young even to me at the time, he was dead. How could that be?

I didn't casually fancy him, because I didn't (and still don't) do anything casually; I was head over heels. James Dean was my gateway drug to becoming a cinephile, an honest-to-goodness movie geek. I avidly watched '50s melodramas and Marlon Brando films. I learned the names of directors such as Elia Kazan and Nicholas Ray. I'll always owe Dean – and maybe my adolescent hormones – a debt for it. There are greater stars, better actors, arguably sexier men; his juvenilia and overt anguish don't do it for me now as they did then. It doesn't matter. I still love him. What this instilled in me, as a moviegoer and eventually as a professional film critic, is just how much male beauty – and frankly, sex – is inextricable from my relationship to some of the movies I love best. What I would come to learn is that wasn't only me who felt this way.

Nearly all of us have yearned for distant dreams on the screen. It might be a young Leonardo DiCaprio tossing around his straw-coloured hair, Eva Green's full-frontal nudity in Bernardo Bertolucci's *The Dreamers*, the flood of internet fandom around heartthrob actor Timothée Chalamet, or an obsession with the hypersensual lesbian cat and mouse game of the BBC's hit show *Killing Eve*. What was your pleasure? We all had one. This isn't exactly remarkable.

From books to movies to theatre, we look to culture to understand who we are, what we can and should become, what conventional happiness looks like, or what ideal personhood is. What desire looks like—both the objects of our desire and the act of being desirous. Even if that desire itself is not explicitly sexual, it's what keeps us striving and dreaming about what it is we want in life; the urge to possess beauty.

No art form is so lushly capable of presenting us what we desire; is as literally dreamlike as cinema. In its stream of transmitted images, stitched together using suggestive editing and montage techniques, it is deeply persuasive and emotionally arresting. For this reason, movies have long influenced the way we think about sex. For women, those formative crushes often give us room to think about our more unspoken desires or preferences in a safe environment, communing with the fiction playing out on screen. For some women (including me) it's a rare comfortable space to explore a relationship with desire. Films are a dream space, allowing room for elaborate sexual fantasia neither as blunt nor as frowned upon as pornography. It's the reason why fanfiction exists, why teen pinups and matinee idols are reliable bellwethers for every generation's adolescence. From Rudolph Valentino to Marilyn Monroe to Chris Hemsworth, they've been with us for a century. Even if the desires we bring home from the cinema are chaste and romanticised, or more about a set of embodied values (for me, Dean's ineffable cool and suburban alienation did this) they make deep, lasting impressions.

Loving movie stars also means loving to look without having to be looked at. In other words, voyeurism is the cornerstone of moviegoing. In the real world, being a woman always means being looked at, even when you don't especially want to be. It means being a tourist in your own body, always self-aware, always a little bit vulnerable. To stare in the safety of the dark is to forget your own hang-ups, your own vulnerability, as many a movie buff will attest to.

Although film holds a curious power over the way society views what is sexually attractive, it's important to acknowledge also has primarily been a vehicle for straight white male sexual fantasy—from a wriggling Jean Harlow circa 1932 to a pert Margot Robbie being condescended to and salivated over in a 2016 *Vanity Fair* profile. Women have rarely been allowed to be on the other side of this equation; to be effusively desirous. Maybe it's because we've been too busy trying to deflect or kowtow to the consistent, piercing gaze of men.

That's true in life as much as it is in art. Living in a woman's body means not being able to talk openly about the experience of being in a woman's body—from talking about menstruation, miscarriages, menopause, sexual violence and yes, sexual desire. But we do desire. Of course we do. And although the 20th century has seen enormous social change in terms of what we are and are not "allowed" to talk about, discussions around female sexuality and female desire have progressed neither as far nor as quickly as we would like.

In 1918, when Marie Stopes published her sex manual *Married Love* with its emphasis on female pleasure, some women in rural parts of Britain had still not been walked through the most basic "facts of life" before childbirth. It was 1968 before radical feminist Anne Koedt's book *The Myth of the Vaginal Orgasm* gave instructions on where the clitoris was. It was 1993 before all 50 states in the US would completely ban marital rape. The Victorian invention of a medical condition known as "hysteria" was used to explain female sexual repression (the term derives from the Greek word for "uterus"). And in 2012, US Republican politician Todd Akin asserted that women are rarely impregnated by rapists because 'the female body has ways to try to shut that whole thing down.' From benign ignorance to rank misogyny, we've had a lot to contend with where our bodies are concerned.

After a century of mainstream cinema, with few exceptions, the representation of female desire on screen has been equally fraught. We see women who are the objects of desire but rarely do we see actively desirous or promiscuous woman characters in a film that gives her agency and respect. We are ogled, objectified and dominated. Even women characters who are ostensibly sexually liberated, like *Fatal Attraction's* bunny-boiling homewrecker Glenn Close, are often punished or treated with thinly veiled disdain.

Our sexuality has been seen as the territory of ridiculous man-eaters and psychotic connivers, in films as variant as '90s erotic thrillers like *The Last Seduction* or '50s dramas a la Douglas Sirk's *Written on the Wind*, where Dorothy Malone plays a "nymphomaniac" nearly destroyed by her own overwhelming impulses. Rather than being allowed their humanity, women are often used as metaphors; as vessels for men's stories or the lessons they must learn.

That's why it's been so easy to turn us into archetypes: the femme fatale, the manic pixie dream girl, the girl next door, the cool girl and countless other iterations of womanhood borne from male fantasy rather than reality. Our bodies are endlessly appropriated by this fantasy and by the male filmmakers who those fantasies belong to. In a seminal 1975 essay, "Visual Pleasure and Narrative Cinema", film scholar Laura Mulvey coined the term "male gaze" to describe this. She wrote that women were traditionally presented as passive – there to be looked at – whereas men were active viewers and protagonists.

In Alfred Hitchcock's *Rear Window* (1954), a male voyeur peeks into women's apartment windows as they go about their daily lives, but we're not meant to care about them; it's him we're invested in. This gendered difference is clear in almost any film noir of the '40s—where the sexy (even predatory) woman was presented both for visual enjoyment and as an untrustworthy figure. The righteous, easily duped Burt Lancaster and the slinky, two-timing dame Ava Gardner in *The Killers* (1946) make for a striking dichotomy along these lines.

As Mulvey has it, audiences are encouraged to enjoy the physical attributes of these women, yet identify with the male protagonist on the screen. Most women are probably so used to identifying with male movie heroes that they hardly think about it. After all, we have no trouble identifying with Iron Man or Indiana Jones, rather than their (fairly cursory) female love interests, such as Gwyneth Paltrow or Karen Allen. Little girls are more likely to want to be these male heroes than their screen girlfriends; to emulate their adventurous masculinity; to dress up as them for Halloween. Frankly, it's hard to feel much of anything for their female counterparts, whose personalities barely seem to register by comparison. (This is probably why, in 2017, so many people were thrilled by Gal Gadot as Wonder Woman). Along those lines, Laura Mulvey rightly points out a patriarchal separation in what we see on our screens: typically, a separation between decorative women and action-oriented men.

Put simply, women's desires and sexual needs are marginalised in movies because they are in real life. Yet cinema offers us the chance to bring women's roles as sexual beings, moviegoers and creators of cinema into sharper focus.

At the moment, many people are discussing women, sex and the film industry, but these topics have been central in all the worst ways. The #MeToo movement, which gained momentum following the 2017 sexual assault and rape allegations against producer Harvey Weinstein, is only a more widespread permutation of decades-long abuses in the film and entertainment world. Even the golden-age dream factory of MGM in the *Wizard of Oz* era essentially pimped out contracted starlets to executives—as depicted in the documentary *Girl 27* (2007). Women in the film industry have historically been victims, collateral damage, casting couch survivors—underpaid and discarded after a perceived sell-by date.

Drowning as we are in the grim litany of sex abuse scandals and draconian shutdowns of women's reproductive rights, the political situation which confronts feminists today is urgent and alarming. It's naïve to assume art can save us, but it can allow us to have difficult conversations—ones made less awkward through the thin veil of fiction. Other lives and possibilities are made accessible through the collective viewing experience of the movies. So the writers in this book will ask: can movies both shelter us from the madness and give us the tools needed to articulate our bodies' deepest needs?

More than that, how can cinema be a place to talk about desire on our own terms? It's clear that as women audience members, it can be tough for us to figure out how and who we relate to up there on the silver screen—if we can relate or identify at all. Anyone who isn't white, cis, able-bodied or heterosexual often fails to see themselves represented on screen altogether, their desires sidelined by mainstream cinema. I want women and nonbinary people of any sexual orientation to rally around cinema as a source of discussion and expression of sexuality that is not anchored in our fraught contemporary reality. This exploration can't be purely, idealistically sex-positive, because that's not the world we live in—or even the world most movie characters live in. If films are a reflection of the societies and eras that wrought them, that can mean they have often given us a mirror into our ugliest and most regressive impulses.

Nonetheless, it's also true that cinema is changing for the better in some corners. Today, more women are writing and directing films than ever before, and telling stories that represent a broad range of female experiences. Everything from Hollywood comedies like *Girls Trip* (2017) to South American indie films like *A Fantastic Woman* (2017) are becoming more inclusive. The former focuses on female friendship and joyous, consequence-free casual sex; both things black women have been denied in cultural representation. The latter, about a transgender woman grieving the death of her older lover, treats sex and love between trans people with the utmost tenderness.

Television, which likely deserves a whole volume to itself, has also moved leaps and bounds ahead: from Jill Soloway's *I Love Dick* to Phoebe Waller-Bridge's *Fleabag*. In both of these shows, the female perspective is prioritised, and women's dirtiest-minded and "inappropriate" impulses are pushed to the fore. In the former, protagonist Kathryn Hahn writes filthy but undelivered letters to the object of her affections (her husband's boss) and the very act of expressing herself, even in secret, gives her newfound swagger. In *Fleabag*, Waller-Bridge (the writer and star of the show) masturbates to an Obama speech and makes asides to the camera as though she and the audience are in on the same joke (and often, that joke is: men.)

Despite these welcome advances, women makers are still only a small proportion of the film industry. According to

The Center for the Study of Women in Television and Film, women directors made up only 20 per cent of directors as of 2018. That's an increase from the previous year, but still pretty paltry. As far as plaudits go, only five women have ever been nominated for Best Director at the Academy Awards. Of those five, only one (Kathryn Bigelow) has won.

Pressingly, the conversation around cinema and television is also still dictated by its male-dominated press corps; the same organisation counts two male film reviewers for every one woman as of early 2019. As a result, even when female-centric, sexually frank material is being produced, there's often a lag in terms of engaged and comprehensive discussion of it in mainstream media.

Yet the more I learned about cinema, the clearer it became that desire is the burning centre of all those flickering images. It seemed that desire could offer a chance at connection in movies not made for women like me, or for women at all. It could help me to understand an actor's stardom, persona and performance. Sex is coded into the DNA of the movies.

As a fledgling journalist, however, I learned to put those thoughts in a locked box. I was busy working my way up to bylines at *The Guardian*, *Sight & Sound*, *VICE* and others. I was attending film festivals and building relationships with colleagues, joining panels and public speaking events, gaining experience in everything from celebrity profiles to investigative research; I wanted to be a professional (whatever that entailed).

Even a few years ago, film criticism was more populated than it currently is by older white men. In a critical context, to talk about sex in relation to movies put me in an uncomfortable position. It highlighted my sexual and gendered difference from the men I was surrounded by—something that already seemed glaring, given my penchant for makeup, for fashion and, frankly, for being conventionally feminine. The unspoken message was that it's unseemly to ogle a handsome man in a film review (even if male reviewers did it to women constantly, and even if that ogling revealed something meaningful about how audience members related to screen stars). Not just unseemly, it was in fact unprofessional, essentially girlish and stereotypically feminine in all the negative ways that women writers do not want to be thought of in a male-dominated news industry.

As much as we're starting to make room for hungrily, even joyously yearning woman (see: *Carol*, *Magic Mike XXL*, *Blue is the Warmest Color*, or *Diary of a Teenage Girl*, all films that have hit the screen since 2010), we're also starting to discuss it openly as film critics. This has been demonstrated by a small but significant shift, particularly in online spaces where culture is discussed. Podcasts such as *Thirst Aid Kit*, hosted by Nichole Perkins and Bim Adewumni, picks through the relative merits of men such as Chris Evans and John Cho, allowing for effusive lusting in a public sphere (with unsurprising amounts of online backlash over "horny women" in the hyperserious, traditionally male world of cultural commentary).

SHE FOUND IT AT THE MOVIES is about female and/or nonbinary filmgoers – whether they be straight or queer, cis or trans – and what they find in the act of looking up at the screen.

The cinema is a safe place for exploring, questioning, dreaming—and sometimes stirring righteous anger. To paraphrase our patron saint Laura Mulvey, perhaps it's crucial to absorb that historical reality, the oppressive dictates of patriarchal movie culture, to look forward to something more radical. Back in the '70s, Mulvey wrote that she hoped we might 'conceive a new language of desire.' That's a worthy challenge, as far as I'm concerned.

As is the way with things deemed taboo, other women I know – professional writers, programmers, festival organisers, filmmakers – seemed thrilled by the prospect of a discussion on female lust in the movies and were eager to share their thoughts.

The writers included in *She Found it At The Movies* are cultural commentators with ideas that feel unwelcome in mainstream media; critical thinkers about the representation of women, bodies and sex in film; activists and changemakers concerned about #MeToo; film industry insiders and outsiders who want to express their lust with both insight and gusto.

Reading these stories about screen desire has taught me a lot: not just about how it's depicted but about how it's interpreted by young queer women, and how cinema can even create obstacles to understanding desire when it does not subscribe to the status quo. These essays are the mere beginning of an exploration of a subject so slippery, so manifold in its dimensions and possibilities, that each writer must speak for themselves. And sometimes, that means reading about desire that we don't understand and can't relate to.

For instance, several years ago, I wrote a piece for *Little White Lies* magazine about a film I loved that I felt didn't love me back: Sam Peckinpah's 1972 crime thriller *The Getaway*. My interest in it was prurient, I suppose; it was regarded as a poorly rated commercial fare from a serious film director. What I couldn't bring myself to admit in the writing of that piece – a piece about how to approach loving a piece of art that was so stridently hateful towards women – was how much my affection for the film was tied up in lively, raw, earnest desire.

The object of that desire is not too surprising. He's a long-dead icon of macho cool and every dad's favourite guy, Steve McQueen. But for a feminist hoping to be taken seriously, that simply was too embarrassing to admit—especially when you consider the facts. McQueen's screen presence is all wrong, for a start. He often plays a chauvinist pig, as he does in *The Getaway*. He'd be the type to reek of stale beer and sweat; the kind of man who'd have you barefoot and pregnant whilst he philandered with a local waitress.

I'm not just talking about the sort of men he played on screen, either; his ex-wife Ali MacGraw admits that, at his behest, she wound up cooking his dinner instead of pursuing her career as an A-list Hollywood actress and tolerating an endless string of infidelities. I know all of this. He was not a nice person. But his promiscuity and his salt-of-the-earth quality make him feel dirtily accessible. Before he was a star, he worked as a marine and – through necessity – a towel boy in a brothel. With his knowing eyes and tanned forearms, he makes me think of bar-room trysts and summertime flings. In short: trouble, but the kind of trouble you'd open your legs for. McQueen is the antithesis of impossible Hollywood fantasy; he's down in the mud with the rest of us. Maybe that's why his image is so sexy.

Loving people on screen that we shouldn't is the subject of more than one of the essays here. What does it mean to be turned on by onscreen abusers and psychopaths, even when in real life you might not touch them with a bargepole? How much room is there in sexual fantasy for political reality? In spite of a relatively recent surge in feminist pornography, made by and for women in ethical circumstances, so much masturbatory fodder remains in one way or another "problematic". Should representation be taken literally, or is it folly to always try to reconcile one's politics with one's sexual pleasures and tastes? Or is choosing to submit to a certain level of domination – and therefore actively picking our fantasy – a feminist act in itself?

Although I'm at some pains to quote the faux-profundity of Jim Morrison, he once wrote that 'film spectators are quiet vampires.' He makes a good point. We seem innocent sitting there in the audience slurping our soft drinks or curled up with our laptops in bed—but our minds are ticking over. We're searching for sustenance, for the most potent elements, and we discard the rest when it doesn't suit us.

In machismo-heavy genre movies, made largely by and for men, I've always revelled in finding something just for me. For women, LGBTQ+ people and people of colour, maybe we can find ways to reclaim white-male-dominated moviemaking as our own. Often that means finding something tiny and sexy in the most unexpected places. Westerns that seem mostly to serve a core audience of "dads" yield for me the slow walk of a Gary Cooper or the sun-browned marble-sculpted visage of Clint Eastwood. It turns out I'm not the only one harbouring secret attractions in strange places.

Throughout this book, the writers ask similar questions. How do we smuggle secret sexy things out of the most innocent of movies? Is it a form of perhaps unhelpful escapism to do so? Yet for others, being a cinephile isn't enough to paper the cracks they see. What if you're nonbinary and it feels nearly impossible to find yourself on screen at all? Or a trans woman who is more likely to see a body like hers depicted in science fiction than in romantic comedy?

Just as we find sex where it was perhaps not intended to be, or where it's inappropriate somehow to acknowledge, there is also a section of films that seem to be shockingly encouraging of these dirty thoughts. Many mainstream action movies borrow from the visual language of beefcake and bodybuilding culture, a tradition born in the 1950s and often intertwined with homosexuality. Hardbodied machos in mainstream movies sometimes turn up in thunderingly obvious moments where gawping at the hunks on screen disrupts the narrative.

Take Roland Emmerich's *Universal Soldier* (1992), featuring the Bob Mizer-like bodybuilder frames of Dolph Lundgren and Jean-Claude Van Damme. It's written into the plot that these supersoldiers occasionally suffer body temperature meltdowns and have to strip off and jump into ice baths or die. This makes for some truly tongue-in-cheek moments, but also allows everyone to ogle. Emmerich, a gay man, does the superviolent action thriller a service by being so boldly subversive.

Whether there are little breadcrumbs left by clever filmmakers or we surreptitiously find them ourselves, there's a lot to be said about the lustful ingenuity of the female moviegoer. It's been said, written and sermonised in a million ways:

women aren't "turned on" in the same functional physical ways that men are, that our sources of desire and pleasure are less built around pornographic visuals than they are a more ephemeral mood or feeling. In spite of recent scientific studies that suggest there's no gender divide in visual pleasure, it's a persistent canard.

Bret Easton Ellis, the author of *American Psycho*, has made his thoughts known on the subject. In spite of having his most famous novel adapted by a female director, Mary Harron, he has said, 'I think it's a medium that really is built for the male gaze and for a male sensibility,' and that where women's arousal was concerned, 'I don't think women respond that way to movies; it's just not how they're built.'

She Found it at the Movies is about proving him wrong. It features 21 culture writers – female and nonbinary – writing about their yearning and why that yearning has revolutionary potential. Desire is a quicksilver thing; ragged, forever shifting. It's as subjective as our love for cinema, and to do it any kind of justice begged for this project to be a collection of voices, not just my own. It needed to be open to a variety of perspectives, sexualities and bodies. The essays within are strident, thoughtful, righteous and often funny exercises in female hunger. A positive rejoinder to all that has made sex and women's sexuality ugly and detested, this anthology seeks to centre it and to rid us of the taboos around it.

In 1965, film critic Pauline Kael published an early collection of reviews that soon became a major text for film buffs and serious cinema devotees. She called it *I Lost it At the Movies*, and in one of her essays on the juvenile delinquent craze in American cinema she wrote about heartthrob *du jour,* James Dean. She described him in evocative, sensual language, harnessing her prowess as a critic to (yes) gawk at him. I can relate. Kael offered spot-on insights into the physicality, sexual chemistry and romantic qualities of the leading men she wrote about—from Cary Grant to Sylvester Stallone. She knew that actors could be both canvasses and tools, that the placement of their bodies in space was meaningful, that a gesture or glance could be everything. To ignore this is to ignore the lifeblood of movies.

At her best, Pauline Kael could combine the knowledge of the finest cinema scholar with the simmering passion of a woman who understood the more voluptuous pleasures of the art. She may have lost something at the movies, but if she's anything like the writers in this anthology, she found something, too. Something rich and full of vitality, fiercely sexy and uncomfortably tender; something it was safe to carry around on repeat in the real estate of your head. For me it was Dean, that insolent blue-eyed man-child. For you, someone else entirely. No matter. It's not about what you find. It's about finding it.

INNOCENCE AND EXPERIENCE

SAINT RIZZO
Sarah Elizabeth Adler

EVERY WEEKEND during my late childhood, I would stand in line at the video store and keep my eyes in front of me. To my left, behind a curtain and down a few steps (though I could never be certain how many), was where they kept the pornography.

Sometimes, when my father was busy at the register, I would let my eyes flit to the sign above the curtain: ADULTS ONLY, 18+, XXX.

Already I had the sense that to be seen entering or exiting that little room – even to be seen looking too long in its direction – would betray some fundamentally humiliating level of need.

Besides, I had my own pleasure to attend to. I was going to rent *Grease* (1978). The name itself felt adult and at the edge of decency. Grease like pomade, like the black oil lubing up a car engine. Grease like pimples, like cheap pizza, like sweat. Grease like sex or, at least, sex appeal.

I first saw *Grease* at a sleepover in the third grade, and it soon became my weekend companion. For years I watched the summer romance between unlikely sweethearts Sandy and Danny get awkwardly resurrected when, unbeknownst to each other, the two return to the same high school for their senior year. Wholesome Sandy has more in common with the bland jocks and student council busybodies than with Danny's foul-mouthed greaser pals and their girlfriends—but by the end of the school year, the star-crossed pair is back together, happily reunited.

Grease was not a movie about my generation or even my parents' generation, and so its cultural references were mostly lost on me. It didn't really matter. I was transfixed by the social topography of senior year at Rydell High, the Kodachrome world of the T-Birds and Pink Ladies, and the pains of adolescence in light of the turbulent social norms of the late 1950s.

Now, of course, I know those pains are more inherent to ages 13 through 19 than to any era in particular. Perhaps this helps explain cinema's enduring fixation with teenagers. Onscreen adolescence is an eternal becoming, a vista from which children conjure the future and adults the past. When I watched *Grease*, I yearned to become.

THERE IS A NOTION, popular among queer people, that if you take a flea comb to the memories of your childhood and teenage years you'll find all the clues to your grown-up sexuality neatly waiting. I have never found this to be a particularly useful exercise. My adult queerness has never felt intelligible in terms of past omens, or like something that could be reverse-engineered from the debris of memory into proof of present identity. I never really wanted the wrong things, I just didn't quite want the right ones. Not a perversion, but a lack thereof.

Except—something was telling about the way I watched *Grease* as a kid, about the force of my fascination with the Pink Ladies and their greaser boyfriends, about girls in tight skirts and boys in leather jackets. Now, I think: what are T-Birds and Pink Ladies by any other, gayer names? Butches, of course, and femmes.

Consider this scene from Leslie Feinberg's novel *Stone Butch Blues*. The narrator, a baby butch named Jess, visits a gay bar for the first time and sees:

> [S]trong, burly women, wearing ties and suit coats. Their hair was slicked back in perfect DAs. They were the handsomest women I'd ever seen. Some of them were wrapped in slow motion dances with women in tight dresses and high heels who touched them tenderly. Just watching made me ache with need.

Not coincidentally, Jess comes of age in the 1950s and '60s. Butch-femme and greaser culture are alike, at least aesthetically speaking, in part because they're contemporaneous. But by the time I was a kid, butch-femme had long since gone out of fashion as the organising dynamic of lesbian life, and I had no notion of it.

What I did have was *Grease*, and with it the knowledge that I was a girl who wanted someone's leather jacket around my shoulders and a hand bigger than my own on the small of my back. It didn't need to be a boy, just... someone who was more a boy than me.

Like Kenickie. I loved watching him sit on the bleachers on the first day of school, legs splayed out, jeans cuffed. He's smoking a cigarette and the next one is already tucked behind his ear. (Kenickie-ness, like butchness, is all in the details.) His shirt is light blue, cottony, a little boy's colour under a leather jacket. You can see the crescent of his white socks over the edge of his mean black boots. The soft under the hard. Kind of like how, in the opening sequence, cartoon Rizzo wears a white bra with hearts – hearts! – under her black shirt.

These details thrill me because I view eroticism as a matter of sacred contrasts: the difference between butches and femmes, the baby blue T-shirt under a black leather jacket, the difference between the hardness that someone shows to the world and the secret softness that lurks beneath.

Kenickie taught me, moreover, about the way that attraction feels geometric: a tug towards the width of someone's shoulders, the lop-sidedness of a grin, the square of a palm. The possibility of a rough hand that, instead of hurting, caresses. The sex appeal of greasers, of butches, and of masculinity in general has a Hippocratic logic. First, do no harm—though you could.

And Rizzo. God. Leader of the Pink Ladies. She's the patron saint of brunettes, of hard girls, of seniors who show up on the last day of school wearing black pencil skirts and red lipstick. Rizzo who, fighting with Kenickie, shows up to the school dance in a red dress with black polka dots and his rival on her arm. Who drives a pink car the same colour as her jacket, the one that says "Pink Ladies" on the back.

Rizzo was nasty, Rizzo was sharp. Rizzo was a girl like me, with a mean streak running right down the middle of her. You say, 'Bite the weenie, Riz' and she says, 'with relish' and smiles with her tongue between her teeth. Ask her what she thinks of the new girl, Sandy, and she knows right away: she looks too pure to be pink.

She knew all the ways that could make someone too pure to be pink. She sings about most of them: no drinking, no smoking, no Elvis. But also, something darker. Watching *Grease* as a teenager, I felt that Rizzo knew, like I did, about what Sandy clearly didn't. She knew about the crude edges of womanhood and the consequences of being too brazen; about the borders where sex and cruelty meet.

Yet even as I love Rizzo, I don't always know what to make of her. Is she a testament to the idea that, if you can't – or don't want to – embrace the sort of femininity expected of you, you can stake out another kind entirely? Or is her sly confidence self-protective, a way to hide the depth of her need?

MY FIRST GIRLFRIEND was the sort of person who could cast away, at once and forever, any social expectation that didn't suit her. She was a rebel, and charming—a total Kenickie dyke. She'd hate me saying that; would never tolerate being compared to a man. (She never called herself butch either, though she knew she was to me).

When I met her she had half a shaved head and the other half was long and black and the most beautiful hair I had ever seen. The soft right next to the hard. She lived in boots and jeans and a leather jacket. She smoked the same cigarettes as my father and had just come back from Paris. The first thing she ever told me was that I looked so French.

At that point in my life, I wore red lipstick and black outfits with lace underneath. I had built a beautiful hard gleaming surface and was waiting for someone – her – to praise and then dismantle it, to undo me.

The calculus of my attraction was whirring and it knew our geometry, how much broader her shoulders were than mine, how much deeper her voice, how much more she knew about tender-bodied things. I wanted desperately to be in relation to her: pressed up against, promised to, opened up underneath. It was a fundamentally humiliating level of need, but it didn't matter. I loved her before we ever touched.

She loved *Grease* too. At least, she liked it well enough. I don't think we ever watched it together, but we sang all sorts of duets. Once we did the penultimate song, the one where Danny and Sandy show up at the school carnival to reunite and declare their love for once and for all:

> Are you sure?
> Yes I'm sure down deep inside.
> You're the one that I want…
> You are the one I want…
> Ooh, ooh, ooh, honey.

Perhaps this is the problem with Danny and Sandy—who are the most prominent yet least-interesting characters. Their reunion makes narrative sense (*Grease* is, after all, a musical) but its inevitability leaves me wanting. It feels at odds with the precariousness of love. The movie ends with them riding off blissfully into the sunset, much like it begins with them kissing on the beach, music swelling in time with the ocean waves that crash to shore.

Compare this to Rizzo and Kenickie, curled around each other in the backseat of his car. Their mood is not one of meek beach kisses. He has a condom, but it breaks. A long pause. And then, Rizzo turns to him. She knows the stakes, and she proceeds in spite of them.

Should this strike me as stupid? It is, but it doesn't. All the things that Rizzo desires – Kenickie, sex, pleasure for pleasure's sake – are treacherous, and she desires them anyway. There are, as she'll sing later, worse things she could do.

For now, in the car, she has one last request. 'Could you call me by my first name?' Kenickie hesitates because he doesn't know it; of course he doesn't, because her surface is hard and gleaming and beautiful.

'Betty,' she tells him. 'Betty.'

This is the moment the surface splits open. She wants him to say her real name, wants to be known under the red and the black and the pink. She wants to hear the truth of things in the true moment, and for him to deliver her to it.

What is sex – the real, good kind of sex, the kind you might be tempted to call making love in spite of yourself – except a mutually arrived-at truth? It's deliverance. It's a circumstance in which you are liberated from yourself, to yourself. It's the pleasure of annihilation.

In college, still waiting for that kind of deliverance, I had a gold nameplate necklace made for myself. It said "Femme". I was taken with the idea of a token with conditions, of one that you could only read if you got close enough to me. Not everyone would understand, of course, but those who got it, I figured, would get it. Those who got it would stand a chance of getting me.

I'd like to think it's the sort of thing that Rizzo would wear, too. A gold chain against a black shirt under a pink jacket. It could say "Pink Lady", or "Riz". Or maybe: "Betty".

PUSH IT REAL GOOD:
HOW 'SET IT OFF' SET IT STRAIGHT
Corrina Antrobus

"A LADY IN THE STREETS and a freak in the sheets" was once more an aspirational mantra for me than a chauvinist R&B lyric. Eventually, such poetics from the likes of Usher and Christopher "Ludacris" Brian Bridges hardwired in me an obedient understanding that a black woman's body was there to service a man's needs. My early visions of black women on screen were pruned with highly sexualised, anonymous "bitches" pumped through music videos where the camera dipped beneath the collarbone and just above the thigh. Little airtime was granted to the face other than to run a wet tongue along a gaping mouth, or to toss a mascara-clad wink to the fourth wall. These women were objects of lust— doe-eyed dolls, dutifully swaying back and forth like rocking horses with no will or desire of their own.

Salt-N-Pepa's "Push It" music video gave me my first throb between the thighs. Cheryl James, Sandra Denton and Latoya Hanson were demanding sex and came with very

specific instructions: *C'mon girls, let's show these guys...*
The audacity stunned me into arousal as they demanded "it"
should be pushed "real good". I didn't know what "it" was,
but this invasion of desire gave me new fantasies. Yet being
turned on made me feel guilty, and masturbation didn't seem
like the kind of thing nice girls did. To satisfy these urges
without a man's assistance was a sin.

My other examples of black female sexuality catered to a
narrow, heterosexual and lecherous gaze. Thanks to the rad-
icalism of Channel 4, there was one black music show, *Flava*,
offering 25 minutes of R&B videos. These were decorated with
mute, voluptuous women. In accessory to the music videos,
there were copies of hip-hop mags *The Source* and *Vibe* read
by giggly boys drooling over women plump in all the right
places. Then there was a friend's dad's porn stash carelessly
rammed behind pirated VHS tapes and Nigerian home movies that we would watch, rigid, with our ears cocked to the
door. We were spellbound by the pudgy nakedness, gyrating
around badly lit bedrooms. The women were open-mouthed,
gasping at something between pain and ecstasy.

All this sex education left me – a twiggy mixed-race girl
with more curls than a pack of Quavers – scorching my hair
straight and shoving what little I had on my chest closer to
my chin. It also carved out an expectation of what I should
prepare myself for when it came to finally "knocking boots"
(as H-Town so sweetly put it). Most of all, it internalised the
idea that a man's gratification – not mine – was all the sexual
self-esteem I could expect.

My visions of the black experience were enriched after
making friends with classmates who had access to cable television and a VHS player. Here I discovered a blossoming era

of '90s black films: *Friday, Poetic Justice, House Party, The Wood, Soul Food, Boomerang, Love Jones, Love & Basketball.* Best of these, though, was a 1996 all-female bank heist drama called *Set It Off*, directed by F. Gary Gray, which I can thank for stoking my fires beyond that Salt-N-Pepa epiphany.

In *Set It Off*, a brief sex scene shows Stony (Jada Pinkett Smith) naked and face down, skin shining like a perspiring bottle of Supermalt. Keith (Blair Underwood), the unfairly handsome black banker, tugs a beaded necklace through the crevice of her magnificently orbed backside and a radiant smile blossoms across her face. We see Keith's face seize with joy as he mouths a moan to the pleasure he's receiving, but also – more importantly – giving. Stony's eyes sparkle and a wall of perfect teeth shine as she drinks in the ecstasy of his service.

Yet the foreplay between "hood" girl Stony and her banker bedfellow begins way before they get creative with a necklace. From the moment they meet, he gets tactile with her mind before he does so with her body. After some impressively corny wooing, Keith persuades Stony to be his date for an office ball. They arrive in a limo and Stony steps out with a demure makeover that Keith brazenly funds. Stony's tightly chained braids are now swept into an updo and for the first time in the movie, we see her face—exposed and liberated. Her lover has freed her butterfly from the cocoon of her class as she becomes a black Cinderella. The fancy soiree sees her removed from her comfort zone of shady LA, and she nervously chugs champagne to ease herself in.

Later, they stand on a balcony, Romeo and Juliet style, looking over the extravagant party and asking each other 'Do you feel free?' For Stony, this is where her tantalisation intensifies. The depth of this conversation penetrates the neglected sensuality of the mind.

Fade to Keith's candlelit bedroom and the wicked chord changes in the sultry strums of En Vogue's "Don't Let Go, Love". The scene reveals Stony finally allowing herself to be pleasured by someone worthy of her body and, unlike with her other sexual partners, the gratification is reciprocal. Elsewhere in the film, she is shown using her body transactionally for her brother's college fund but with Keith, these power dynamics don't exist.

Stony's scene of unadulterated pleasure unbuttoned years of conditioning that black women lack, or don't deserve, sexual agency. In that one silky moment, it confirmed that they can be in charge of their sexual desires and deserve satisfaction. Stony also reframes a vision of sex appeal; she never looks sexier than when driving into the sunset in jeans, a white vest and a shaved head. This is sexier than the makeover Keith arrogantly curates. It was the revelation I didn't know I needed.

Set It Off tore down and rebuilt what sexy looked like throughout. Dressed in oversized jeans and tablecloth-style shirts, the cast (Jada Pinkett Smith, Queen Latifah, Vivica A. Fox and Kimberly Elise) looked as curvy, elegant and powerful as the trigger of a gun. The film unwittingly confirmed that black women's bodies are not there to serve a white man's sexual bucket list or pander to a rapper's ego.

A dozen years later, Pinkett Smith continues to affirm that a black woman can surrender to sexual fantasy whilst receiving love and respect. In *Magic Mike XXL* (2015), she plays the wanton sex goddess Rome; as Lisa in *Girls Trip* (2017) she actively pursues a handsome younger man. Along with nuggets such as the deflowering scene in Barry Jenkins' *If Beale Street Could Talk*, Taraji P. Henson's boss lady role in the hysterical *What Men Want*, and rapper Khia's lyrics (demanding you lick her pussy and her crack), these moments address the lack of wider representations of black female sexual empowerment since *Set It Off*.

But let's not mistake an inch for a mile. The eventual tragedies in *Set It Off* make deeming this film "empowering" debatable. It's important to detect the pitfalls of the male gaze, even in films like this one. There are many well-meaning attempts to radicalise onscreen female sexuality, but they are often filtered through a patriarchal worldview. Exhibit A is Spike Lee's 1986 *She's Gotta Have It*, which sees the cocksure Nola liberally sharing her bed with a variety of men. Feminist writer bell hooks critiques Nola's sexual gusto as being framed as "abnormal" and verging on mental disorder. Here hooks states: 'Her sexual fulfilment is never the central concern. She is pleasured only to the extent that she is able to please.' And as Mars (one of Nola's friends with benefits) says: 'All men want freaks [in bed]. We just don't want them as a wife.' Perhaps this is a confession of the internalised patriarchy of a young Spike Lee. It certainly looks ahead to the beliefs of the Ludacrises of the world.

Black bodies are still suffering from institutional racism and the history of absurd pseudoscience, where sexuality was seen as a key metric of social behaviour. Throughout his work, historian Sander L. Gilman has examined the way in which misinformed notions of sexual conduct came from dreaming up arbitrary standards to measure the evolutionary attainment of different races. These were often based on genitalia size and the more nebulous "sex drive". The resulting scale placed Africans at the bottom and white Oxbridge-educated men at the top, which will surprise approximately no one.

Film critic Cameron Bailey riffs on these findings he brands as "Hottentot" in a 1987 copy of radical film critique magazine *CineAction!*: 'It was deduced that the black female possessed not only a primitive sexual appetite but also the external signs of this temperament: "primitive" genitalia. Enlarged labia, big buttocks and monstrous penises loomed large in the 19th-century scientist's imagination as fearsome signifiers of animal-like hypersexuality that was threatening in its force.' The inability to comprehend or accept difference led to slanted research which at best alienates and at worst poses a physical threat. In her book *Monstrous Intimacies*, Scholar Christina Sharpe notes that the 'construction of black women as uninhibited in their sensuality made the black female body a seemingly logical place for white men to "sow their wild oats".'

When it comes to adequate and authentic representations of black female experience in cinema, we're still falling short—hardly a surprise when so few of them get the opportunity to express their reality on the big screen. Unsurprisingly, the authorship of black women provides a riper depiction of their own sexuality. Gina Prince-Bythe Wood's *Love & Basketball* provides a considered female gaze when Sanna Lathan's character chooses to lose her virginity to her child-hood sweetheart. Dee Rees' masterful *Pariah* sees Adepero Oduye's leading character carefully engage with her queer-ness; Michaela Coel's hilariously horny role in TV's *Chewing Gum* and Issa Rae's *Awkward Black Girl* welcome black women in on the fun.

From confessional ignorance to unashamed thirst, these examples flesh out surface-level assumptions based on skin. They decolonise lazy assumptions which see black women reduced to exoticism. They've also helped me re-evaluate those early lessons that were pumped from the organs of mass media. On some level, I think they had me somehow looking forward to being sexually oppressed and forcing myself into the mould of white beauty ideals.

It's both a disservice to society and a warning alarm that films directed by black women are still so limited in number. For black women in the audience, the opportunity to relish in that work helps to strengthen a sense of identity, create compassion and enhance sexual self-esteem. This can only occur through nuanced representations that black women themselves can provide. Carrying the torch sparked by the flint of *Set It Off*, I'm now enlightened enough to know that sexual satisfaction should be reciprocal—and that my mind is just as much an erogenous zone as my body.

'THE SOUND OF MUSIC' IS THE
HOTTEST FILM I'VE EVER SEEN

Anne Rodeman

I'M THE YOUNGEST, loudest and least-baptised thing to come out of my parents' 47 years of marriage. My brother and sister got plunged out of respect for the extended German Catholic families of the 1970s that my parents were both trying to appease. But by the time I was born, they were ready to let go of the last vestiges of familial religious obligations. I grew up realising that we very much did not believe in god and that the relatives very much prayed for us on Sundays. This isn't to say my childhood didn't consist of open-casket funerals, two-hour wedding ceremonies and five-hour fish fries. Even for us, Catholicism loomed large. We popped in for the family's big life events because even former Catholics usually make a big deal out of birth, marriage and death. Of my maternal grandmother's eight daughters, five of them entered the convent. Of those five, four would eventually leave. One became a psychologist; one moved back home after she finished high school; one was forced to leave after a suicide attempt; one left after a year of silence to become a poet, teacher and my mother. The one who is still there, the last remaining nun in my family, is Aunt Patricia—Pat for short.

When I was a kid, Pat lived in St. Louis proper with two other nuns, Sister DeLillis and Sister Mary Joseph in a beautiful old house. Some days Pat would walk us to the convent where I got to play Marco Polo with the other nuns in the heated pool, or we would watch the St. Louis Cardinals baseball games in high definition because the nuns had chipped in to buy an enormous plasma-screen TV for their common room. Other days, when I was bored by the chit-chat over Aunt Pat's tomato plants out back, she would set me up with Ritz crackers, a Coke, and the extensive VHS collection she had compiled from years of recording off late-night television. Somewhere amidst the Bobby McFerrin PBS pledge drives there was treasure to be discovered: *The Wizard of Oz, Mary Poppins, Singin' in the Rain* and *The Sound of Music*. I fed this quartet of masterpieces into her cranky VCR, spurring a lifelong love of musicals and an aching desire to know Julie Andrews.

As an adult, the opening scene of *The Sound of Music* is the sort of sweeping, unrealistic and unapologetically grand movie-making that makes me weep. A distant whistle echoes as we scan across a stock-still river valley, a patch of mountainside pines, a village nestled between the green and blue hills, a villa, and eventually we rise to find a woman alone in the mighty Alps, atop a knoll, and the whistle swells into a triumphant major chord as she spins into song. I watch *The Sound of Music* at least once a year, and with forty-something viewings under my belt my experience of the film has evolved from entertainment to ritual. And with each annual viewing, the distance between the cross-legged Midwestern child-me (who loved chicken and boys) and the firm-footed grown-up New-Yorker-me (who doesn't entertain either) stretches further into the Missouri landscape. The opening whistle of the film, now ripened with time, memory and place, can elicit full-body quivers in me. But the film also operated on another level, and it wasn't just the musical grandeur and visual beauty of *The Sound of Music* that grabbed me. It was Julie Andrews as the nun-in-training.

Maria, dressed in all that wool. It happens early, as Maria closes the gate to the convent behind her: turned-up nose, honey blond pixie cut, top button buttoned with just a hint of a bodice underneath. She's wearing a stiff-brimmed hat. She is scared but determined, and she looks tall and perfect.

It would be years before I discovered Julie's entirely believable butch energy in the 1982 musical *Victor/Victoria*, or her ideal synthesis of litheness and curves, both of which were on display in *Star!* (1968) thanks to the finale's sequined unitard. And despite my parents' best efforts to keep it at bay, I suppose it might be Catholic shame that has kept me from ever seeing the 1981 comedy *S.O.B.*, in which Julie, as directed by her husband, Blake Edwards, reveals her (reportedly) great rack. *Mary Poppins*, of course, had her own brand of flinty sex appeal. Yet it was Maria, and the knowing glances she shared with her budding protégé, Liesl, that lit my loins all those years.

At eight, I knew enough to clamp a pillow between my thighs and buck back and forth with my eyes closed and the door locked. I was Liesl climbing into Maria's bedroom, sopping wet in a muddied dress. Maria keeps my tawdry Rolf secret, then offers me a hot shower and some of her own clothes to tumble into before the younger children arrive trembling at the foot of the bed. We are lovers leading these frightened youngsters in song and mild pillow play. I gaze into her eyes and say, 'Well, maybe I do need [a governess].' This was formative. As an adult, it is easy to see the direct line between Maria's wry babysitter vibe and my teenage fixations.

There was my slender seventh grade teaching assistant, Ms Grand, who had hair like Peter Pan. I used to flirt with her by writing notes about movies on the homework assignments that I knew she was going to grade. *Did you see 'Norma Jean & Marilyn' last night? I really love Mira Sorvino. Who's your favourite actress?*

I desperately tried to prove my sophistication to a worldly friend who studied abroad her junior year of high school. I sent her volumes of Colette and Angelou with page-length inscriptions and L7 mixtapes with liner note drawings of us reuniting mid-Atlantic.

See also my friendship with a New York character actress who was 15 years my senior. She had moved back to Missouri and was now starring in our community theatre production of *The Wizard of Oz*. I bought her a gas station rose, took it backstage and asked for her email in the hopes she could give me life advice. Or something.

The Sound of Music's clearest primary narrative might be the love story of the Captain and Maria, but for me the

Maria/Liesl mentor/mentee flirtation was the truer arc. Their relationship acted as air traffic control batons, directing my prepubescent eyes and imagination towards the kind of relationship two women might have with one another.

The movie cracked open for me from there and it turns out there was a lot more Catholic-adjacent sex in *The Sound of Music* that neither Aunt Pat nor my parents seemed to be noticing. These children are all crushing hard on their governess and angling to find a way into her bed. Captain Von Trapp fingers a riding crop throughout the film. After the Laendler sequence, Maria blushes in the Captain's face, clearly embarrassed at her own arousal. The Baroness' speaking voice has all the husk and easy confidence you could ask for in a glacially hot, shamelessly manipulative, independently wealthy woman: 'Is there something I can do to help?' Baroness Schraeder is no fool and takes note of Maria's figure not once, but twice: first when Maria emerges from the pond, hips and tits on display, and second when Maria undresses in her bedroom before running away from the clearly soon-to-be sexual affair with Captain Von Trapp.

Drenched in moonlight, the Captain and Maria eventually admit the moment that they first knew they loved each other. His: when she 'sat on that ridiculous pinecone.' Hers: when he first 'blew that silly whistle.' I'm not sure love is the word you're looking for when talking about sitting and blowing, but sure—whatever works. And lest we forget the oestrogen-charged "16 Going on 17" where Liesl sprays her pheromones all over the gazebo whilst letting Rolf think he's teaching her something she doesn't know. By the end of the song, he is ready to kiss and she is ready to fuck.

Only when I asked did my mom tell stories about living through the 1960s at The Mount, the place where the convent and boarding house was located at the top of a St. Louis hill, two and a half hours from her hometown. She had to eat stuffed green peppers and whole milk that had gone off because that was a typical dinner. She played basketball and baseball, and roller-skated in the traditional wool tunic and underskirts, sweating through Missouri summers and late teenage period cramps because pain relievers were prohibited. She had fond memories of the great education and all the singing, less so the year of silence the Novitiate required.

So she left. She went to college, fell in love, had three kids, earned a PhD, wrote poetry, taught for 15 years and built a life rich in words and art. She gave me Libra as a middle name. She took me to *Fiddler on the Roof* when I was four and answered all my questions about pregnancy and blowjobs (we had HBO) when I was nine. When I was 15, she quietly dropped an empty journal and a book by Ellen DeGeneres on my nightstand. And when I came home from college at the age of 21 after not calling for three months, she silently held me in my childhood bed with all the energy of Mother Superior's "What is it you can't face?" pulsing between us for an hour before I breathed the words "I'm gay" into my sheets.

Back at the beautiful old St. Louis house, Aunt Pat sat by her tomatoes in her plainclothes (despite my protestations, I never got to see her in her habit except for in the headshot that resided in St Mary's hospital, where she ran the lab). She served DeLillis, Mary Joseph and my parents pimento dip and Bud Light, had one herself, and slapped her long thigh-bone as she laughed at her favourite joke, which was a pun about a duck and its beady eyes.

That was my cue to retire to the living room with my crackers and my coke. I parked myself on top of a "Faith Moves Mountains" throw pillow and rewound to the bedroom scene, curtains billowing in anticipation of Liesl's arrival.

SEARCHING FOR MARLENE DIETRICH IN BERLIN

Lauren Vevers

BEFORE I KNEW I WAS BISEXUAL, I'd heard of Marlene Dietrich. I saw her portrait on a postcard and I was struck, as I suppose many people are, by her angular bone structure and her facial expression that contained multitudes of soft-ness and of sternness. She was unlike any woman I'd ever seen. There was something about the composition of the image. In the photograph she was shot from below, her stance authoritative and potent. Her androgynous glamour was in equal parts down to her masculine style and her self-assured bearing. The more I learnt about Dietrich, the more I admired her. When she first left Berlin for Hollywood, she was 29 and a mother. Everything about her, at least on the face of it, was bold and assertive.

In the spring of 2018, I was neither of those things, so I decided to take a trip with Marlene Dietrich in mind. I'd come out of a long-term relationship with a man I loved deep-ly and I was stuck in a job I hated. I'd spent most of my life in the city where I grew up because it was comfortable. The thought of solo travel scared me. But I'd felt trapped for so long by the current of my own fears that I knew it was time to make a change. On the plane, I ordered an in-flight gin, for courage.

In Berlin, I take the S-Bahn to the Strandbad Wannsee and walk the tree-lined path to its entrance. Fragments of sunlight dance through the leafy canopy; the weather is unseasonably warm for May. This famous lake has served bathers for over a century. Now a cultural heritage site, it plays host to around a quarter of a million visitors in peak bathing season. When I arrive, everything is still. Two men are lying on beach towels, the curves of their stomachs pink in the heat. A woman applies a generous layer of cream to her breasts. I buy a beer and pay extra for a beach shelter. At some point, my phone buzzes. It's a text from my ex-boyfriend. Despite the months that have passed, we're holding onto the threads of each other. I miss him but at the moment he seems far away. Berlin in spring is full of hope, full of possibility.

Back at my hostel, I half-heartedly download a dating app and set my preferences. Age range 25–35. Men. Women. If you were an actress in the Golden Age of Hollywood, offscreen lesbian affairs were generally considered good for your constitution and onscreen magnetism. Greta Garbo referred to her sexual relationships with women as "exciting secrets". Dietrich married her husband Rudolf Sieber in 1922 and had many extramarital affairs with both women and men over the course of her life. Her daughter, Maria Riva, writes: 'I have never judged my mother for her emotional gluttony, only for the way she treated those who loved her. Occasionally the rapidity of her turnover of bed partners was embarrassing.' How would Dietrich have fared on Tinder? Probably quite well, I think, as matches begin to appear. A shirtless Australian guy on a Contiki Tour. An earnest app developer living in Wedding with his Dachshund. A tattooed barista. Conversations are stilted and forced. I can't get a real sense of anyone I'm talking to, so I take myself out to dinner in an overpriced tapas bar and shelter from the torrential rain. I'm surrounded by couples in candlelight. There's something magical about existing in a city where you have the option to be anonymous and a romance to that type of aloneness. In Berlin, I could be anyone I wanted to be. I turn off my phone, sip my wine and wait for the storm to pass.

In her films, Marlene Dietrich provoked the viewer in roles which subverted expectations of gender norms and sexuality. In *The Blue Angel,* she's a cabaret girl who attracts the attention of a middle-aged professor (played by Emil Jannings). It was one of the first movies of the sound era and was recorded in both German and English, and the film endures today as a seductive tragicomedy. When Dietrich sings "Falling in Love Again" she is coquettish in the role of a coy temptress. On the surface, there's nothing subversive about Lola. But as Professor Rath's lust for her becomes all-consuming, Dietrich's character becomes more powerful than Rath. Lola, thinking he has money to his name, agrees to marry him. When his money runs out, he is forced to work as a clown in a travelling troupe and Lola becomes contemptuous of their relationship, taking other lovers. In the end, Professor Rath is driven mad by jealousy, unable to tame her desire or quell her sexuality. In her next film, *Morocco,* Dietrich plays another cabaret performer where she dresses in a tailcoat and a top-hat—a typically male ensemble. In a room full of legionnaires she eschews advances from men, instead lightly kissing a woman on the lips. In *Morocco*, Dietrich's performance is bolder than in *The Blue Angel*. It's a more explicit demonstration of her sexual potency. Rather than becoming a passive object of desire, she becomes the one pursuing. Even though the kiss itself isn't sexual, the act of the kiss is defiant and bold. It's mesmerising to watch a woman dressed as a man hold the attention of a room full of people. Dietrich is beautiful, although it's not her beauty that makes me return to this scene again and again; I'm attracted to the enviable power and authority of her sexuality.

The Deutsche Kinemathek is an imposing glass building that houses many of Germany's film and television secrets. Sweaty from the U-Bahn, in shorts and a T-shirt and wearing a cheap bra I'd packed in error, I'm self-conscious as I ask the attendant for a ticket. I've always struggled with the way I look. Dietrich embodies a glamour I simply can't emulate. I meander through the exhibits before reaching a mirrored room dedicated to her costumes. Amongst the sparkle and plush fabrics and sharp lines of exquisite tailoring, I see my reflection: short, awkward and uncomfortable in my own skin. Dietrich was known for her glamour. The list of designers she wore is endless, including Christian Dior, Elizabeth Arden, Jean Louis and Travis Banton. She was one of the first women to wear a suit outside the intimacy of private parlours. I have tried many times to reinvent my style, to no avail. Dietrich's charisma extended to her ability to own any outfit from a ballgown to a suit. She once said, 'I am sincere in my preference for men's clothes. I do not wear them to be sensational. I think I am much more alluring in these clothes.' Growing up as a teenager in the North East of England you have a limited number of acceptable choices about how to dress. Fake tan or no fake tan? Hair extensions or no hair extensions? In my late teens, I lived in men's T-shirts and leggings—to the horror of many of my peers who insisted that I wear form-fitting outfits to show off my figure. I liked trousers and shirts and, though I couldn't replicate her poise, discovering Dietrich meant I could justify these choices. Suddenly, it was okay to dress differently and to conflate the binary masculine and feminine rules of fashion.

Dietrich's relationship with Berlin was complex. After the success of *The Blue Angel*, she followed film director and collaborator Josef von Sternberg to Hollywood and rarely returned to her hometown. Before that, she was a regular at the Eldorado, a famous Berlin nightclub, where she featured on the bill with artists and drag performers. It was a space for Dietrich to play with gender presentation, and it was this experimentation that continued to inform her image throughout her career. If Dietrich was a trailblazer in terms of her brazen and visible sexuality, it was Berlin's queer scene that helped her to lay the foundations. We carry with us the cities we were born in; they are sewn into the fabric of who we are as people. Yet I think moving away allowed Dietrich an extra measure of reinvention; to become iconic she had to go to Hollywood where her transgressive style was celebrated for its uniqueness, and where her desire for women could be seen as an extension of her universal androgynous appeal.

My routine on holiday is to get up early and go to a coffee shop where the lights are low-hanging and everything is fashionably sterile. Tinder conversations aside, I haven't spoken to anyone for days. I'm thinking about my ex a lot so it's a welcome interlude when, over breakfast, an old friend messages me on Facebook. She says she's living in Berlin with her boyfriend and asks if I want to meet her. Later that evening, in a restaurant on Bergmannstrasse, we drink rice vodka cocktails and talk about what had happened in the six years since we'd seen each other last. As we talk, I feel a flicker of something like mourning for the experiences I could've had if I'd been brave enough to leave my hometown.

Newcastle is a compact city with a vibrant, if insular, creative scene. Dating casually isn't necessarily an option when there's only a small pool of people who have the same interests and ideologies as you. When you're young, there's a simmering pressure to find a life partner, get a mortgage and settle down. I haven't had the strength to tell my family about my bisexuality and, although my parents are understanding, the constant justification of my life choices to friends and relatives is draining. My last relationship lasted several years. I was sincere in my love for him but I'd been denying my attraction to women. If I'd left, I'd have had more opportunity to explore my desires and I might've been less afraid.

On my last night in Berlin, I dance with my friend in a tiny smoke-filled club until we burst onto the streets and the morning catches us in its arms. On the plane home, groggy and sleep-deprived, I look back at my notes from the last week. I'd set out to find out more about who Dietrich was and in reality, I'd only found contradictions. Understanding her as more than an icon means recognising that, like any person, she was complicated. As much as she appeared to have been fiercely independent-minded, much of her success was tied to von Sternberg; he was responsible for the curation of her image and had strong opinions about how she presented. I'm also cautious about making assumptions around Dietrich's sexuality. She talks openly about relationships with both men and women, but was she bisexual in the modern sense? I don't think it's fair to speculate. All of this is an important reminder that Dietrich was more than a myth. It occurs to me that the women of Old Hollywood are often put on pedestals and that in itself is dehumanising; it means that we're rarely able to think of them beyond the arc of their career and that we don't give them room to be multifaceted or flawed.

When I say I admire Dietrich, what I actually mean to say is that I admire the idea of her, and of what she's come to represent. I enjoy her exoticised glamour, her enigmatic personality and her ability to embrace her sexuality. It hasn't escaped me that I might find her larger-than-life persona appealing because it epitomises everything I believe I'm lacking. Berlin, even with its potential to offer new experiences, didn't have the answer. I've spent most of my twenties searching for something or someone to help abate my loneliness. In looking for external solutions, I never really considered that I was creating a barrier to my own happiness by ignoring what was going on internally. An identity crisis or an eroded sense of self (or whatever you chose to call it) wasn't going to be solved by moving to a new city. In holding Marlene Dietrich up as an example, I was sort of punishing myself by comparing my life to a false ideal. Maybe it was healthier to let her go.

A few months later, back in Newcastle, I go to my local DIY theatre for a series of events celebrating work by LGBTQ+ artists. By chance, part of the showcase is a piece called "Dietrich: Natural Duty"—a drag cabaret act that encapsulates Dietrich's spiky humour and poise. As the house lights go up, I'm emotional. I'd grown up thinking my bisexuality was, at best, inconvenient and at worst, deviant. I'd experienced deep shame about who I was fundamentally and that feeling had stayed with me into adulthood. As the noise from the audience enveloped the room, I was filled with temporary relief. It felt good to be surrounded by warm applause in a welcoming queer space. It felt good to know I was moving towards self-acceptance. For a long time, I believed that people like me didn't belong to a city like this. I'd gone in search of Marlene Dietrich in Berlin, but I'd found her much closer to home.

MURDEROUS FOPS AND
HORNY TEENS
Caroline Golum

GROWING UP IN THE SHADOW of Third Wave Feminism
– caught between the competing impulses of pornographic
moral panic and fomenting "girl power" – it seemed nearly every grownup had me pegged. By the time I'd reached
something resembling maturity and self-awareness, the radical foundation of mid-century women's liberation had been
reshaped. As rocks are shaped by the pounding seas, modern womanhood had been carved into a pair of competing
monuments. On one side: the reactionary modus operandi
of anti-pornography feminists hellbent on exorcising from
our patriarchal society the evils of smut, sex work and trans-
sexuality. Across the aisle: the rapid onslaught of wholesale
empowerment, represented by an increasing reliance on late
capitalism, to shatter our chains.

In that liminal space between the Andrea Dworkins and
Hillary Clintons of the world, a fecund counterculture began
to emerge in the form of 'zines, arthouse films and nascent

blogs touting body-positive bromides and sisterly love advice. Ever the fast-talking hoyden, I found my level in this DIY No Man's Land: "sassy", "lippy", "bossy" and sundry other synonyms for "loud and/or uncompromising" made their way onto my report cards. And why shouldn't they? The daughter of a vociferous working mother, and instructed to speak my mind and behave as I pleased (within reason), my girlhood was the antithesis of that of my forebears in nearly every way. There was no career option too lofty, no opinion ignored. The facetious notion of a gender binary had yet to make its way to the San Fernando Valley circa 1999, so unapologetic tomboyishness became the quickest shorthand I could muster. With my short hair and unfussy wardrobe, I could stand shoulder-to-shoulder with any boy in my class.

We shared our passions, right down the line, save for one crucial difference. To my classmates, I was a sexless playmate—but to me, they were exotic; alluring. I've never doubted my assigned gender, but there was always something about boys (and later, men) that I coveted. Simple penis envy doesn't begin to describe this latent phenomenon—rather, I suspect that my fixation was rooted in some admixture of fear and desire. The rough antics of my male counterparts were at once repulsive and titillating, and those early days were spent attempting, often in vain, to emulate that unnameable quality I so adored. When puberty reared its ugly head, all bets were off: my schoolyard boy-pals became the unwitting quarry of a salivating huntress within.

The severity of this seemingly overnight transformation destroyed those innocent halcyon days and my presence – never crude or jocular enough – at pizza parties and outings to the local multiplex became an unwelcome one. To throw another log on this thirsty fire, I learned early the meaning of self-doubt, self-loathing and self-sabotage. Increasingly, my classroom came to resemble more an abattoir than an incubator of critical thought. At a social and physical nadir, my brain colonised by unmanageable hormones, there appeared to be no end to, or outlet for, my mounting frustration. Humming along, seemingly in parallel, was a burgeoning cinephilia, cultivated by my family over dinner table arguments and Friday night video rentals.

With a taste for the macabre and a deep reservoir of nostalgia, those first steps into the wading pool of moviegoing seemed to mark me for a wholly different fate than that of a would-be "SheEO". Teachers, parents, even kindly older neighbours tried in vain to steer my too-rapid thoughts towards scholarly pursuits and the self-satisfaction of a hard day's work. How could they understand that my world outside the aspect ratio was little more than a laundry list of drudgery? School, then more school, work, then (if I was lucky) an easy death. The alternative universe afforded me by cable television and scant parental oversight was – if you'll pardon the cliché – a sole shaft of light in this otherwise dark phase.

It was a schoolgirl crush on a soft-spoken violin prodigy that lit the spark and set a subsequent fire of perversion that smoulders to this day. I don't remember how it came to pass that this knock-kneed boy became my obscure object of desire but – then, as now – when I fell it was hard and fast. As far as first loves go, I could have done a lot worse: how fortunate that he shared my predilection for classic Hollywood and not something boring (like professional sports). When he divulged this passion to me, I felt every inch the blushing bride, and our first of many home movie dates could not have been better timed.

In the weeks leading up to Halloween, he invited me to go in costume with him as *Psycho's* Norman Bates and Mother: he dressed as the latter, I as the former, adding another Freudian layer to this already befuddling trifle. Somehow, I persuaded my parents to rent the film for me as "research", and my crush and I watched it together in a fog of what I would later recognise as total ecstasy. When Norman Bates appeared on screen, I studied him intently, bewitched by the (perceived) similarities between this quiet, doe-eyed serial killer and my beloved companion.

Another cliché, if I may: the brightest flame often burns the shortest, and my romance was no exception. The shy boy and I took wholly different academic paths, and I fell in with a group of mall goths. Where he rose above the psychic mire of those early obsessions, I threw myself into them head-long, enchanted by the prospect of a black wardrobe and authority-signalling leather accessories. Those appetites – for boys and films in equal measure – increased alongside my bra size, and the process of corruption kicked into high gear. At a too-tender age, I begged for (and received, miraculously) a copy of Anthony Burgess's *A Clockwork Orange*, and through a friend with permissive parents managed to secure an early DVD release of Stanley Kubrick's violent, psychedelic adaptation.

Across a spectrum of intense emotions – reverence, shock, curiosity – my most vivid recollection is a profound and early sense of sexual guilt. Alex DeLarge, played with cheeky foppishness by a young Malcolm McDowell, was as nasty a piece of work as I'd ever seen on screen. Norman Bates was a murderer, sure, but at least he loved his mother—no work of fiction had yet prepared me for the mental gymnastics in which I about to engage. Handsome, eloquent, English; he ticked every box, and charmed me even in the throes of ultraviolence. What could I do but look, unflinchingly, at this preening sadist in shiny black boots and a bulging codpiece? The ever-present possibility of sexual violence – on the street, on dates, or anywhere, it seemed – had yet to take root in my garden of phobias, and some naïve part of me could still separate "man" from "deed". Shameful though it may seem now, the prospect of a night at Korova Milk Bar with this juvenile delinquent tugged my black-lipsticked mouth into a scheming smile.

Still, the twin hungers for male proximity and dollar-bin DVDs continued to grow apace. Yoked to these obsessions like some mindless animal, I trudged up the Everest of my desires towards a summit I couldn't yet picture, one far away from the tenuous present—back in time, back to the Old World. It was a purchase from an aforementioned discount store that nudged me further along my path to perversion, into a craggy forest wrested from the primordial soup of the Brothers Grimm. When, one idle afternoon, I snagged a cheap release of F. W. Murnau's *The Cabinet of Dr. Caligari*, it felt as though I'd stumbled upon a kind of Rosetta Stone, an ur-text for everything I loved about filmcraft and masculinity. Conrad Veidt's kohl-rimmed eyes and hollow cheeks, framed by oily locks of austere black hair—ah, reader, "lust" is too simple a word. This lissom instrument of terror became an avatar for my own conflicting desires: with enough mascara and black turtlenecks, could I transform myself into Murnau's pillow-lipped somnambulist? Or would simply devouring him be enough?

Every now and then, as needed, I came up for air and took stock of my surroundings: still without incident, still floating lazily through the monotony of suburban school life. The days and weeks passed slowly and seemingly without end, bringing with them increasing pressure.

As a young woman, cultivated by the nurturing hand of postwar feminism, my ambitions were unencumbered. In that limitless drive for perfection, I found no satisfaction, only exhaustion. Every schoolgirl pal, it seemed, harboured not-so-secret dreams of becoming the first female American president. Back then, we were still foolish enough to believe that women could do anything, be anything, they wanted—but all I wanted was a black-gloved hand around my neck.

I learned to couch my peccadilloes – fairly harmless in hindsight but, again, this was nearly two decades ago – in the language of armchair academia. Towards my fellow sisters in the struggle, I kept the mask of innate confidence and steely resolve firmly in place. I was studying, you see: to adequately combat a menacing patriarchy, I had to know my enemy from the inside out. Never mind that maelstrom of shame that haunted my idle daydreaming—what would my girlfriends think? Could any man understand, let alone satisfy, these vaguely violent impulses? Surely these perverse notions could (and should) be suppressed. In high school, I started taking birth control – without protest from my family, thankfully – and revelled in this bit of sexual autonomy that felt at odds with my psychic black book of desires. An outspoken believer in women's liberation, I could not reconcile my warring public and private personae. On the surface, I was nobody's fool, impervious to the baser instincts that rapped at the door of my desires. That is until another similarly inclined and similarly proportioned woman laid the answer at my feet.

At eighteen, I was released at last from my ancestral home and let loose upon a teeming metropolis chock full of perverts. Under the marabou-feathered wing of a family friend (a Dutch lifestyle journalist with a fondness for lingerie) those early days of young adulthood were imbued with an overwhelming sense of possibility. Every outing was an occasion. One brisk autumn evening, not long after I left the nest, this kooky woman invited me to a talk at the cavernous SoHo flagship store of Agent Provocateur, where a dominatrix named Anna M. just happened to be lecturing on her unusual trade.

To my great surprise I discovered, contrary to my preconceived prejudices, that the bulk of her clientele was not the meek and mild, but "Masters of the Universe": stockbrokers, CEOs and similarly high-powered individuals. In short, men (mostly) in positions of considerable power, who spent their days deciding the fate of millions of people and dollars. So much depended on these men, poor things, that you could forgive them their desire to be hogtied and flagellated by a stern woman. Relinquishing control was a vacation, of sorts, from the exhaustive task of maintaining a crack-free façade.

Bless Anna M., wherever she is – sleeping on a pile of money, one hopes – for putting so plainly what I couldn't discern myself. In that moment the whole messy, guilt-stricken puzzle of my libido fell into place. Didn't I feel, after years of urging from peers and authority figures, like a budding Mistress of the Universe? More than a sexual hang-up or mere animal lust, the years-long appeal of casual sadism revealed itself to me as a craving more nuanced than I'd previously thought. The apparent bossiness I displayed, my blatant hunger for control – always control – over my own destiny were hallmarks of a type-A personality.

Those cinematic vessels of my girlish desires – lurking across some chiaroscuro screenscape in search of a fresh kill – began to look, in hindsight, like little more than shallow reflecting pools. If my dream partners in these sexual power plays could be forgiven their trespasses, surely I could enjoy the same privilege? In simpler, less liberated times, we celebrated and encouraged these tendencies among our brothers and sons. Men were domineering, but it was women like me that made them that way. Talking out of turn meant a smack in the mouth from a Humphrey Bogart or John Garfield—just my type, it so happens.

I wanted, desperately, to obtain the blessing of authority that maleness conferred, to wallow in the privilege of flexing, fucking up and finding redemption through forgiveness (or punishment). And at the same time, I was a slave to that ambition—I'd bitten off more than I could chew, and my mile-a-minute mentality had grown tired. The need to slip out of my liberated girlpower suit and into something a little more uncomfortable (maybe in black patent leather?) gave me that permission. Someone else could run the show, and I could slide back into the driver's seat when I'd had enough.

Armed with this fresh revelation, unencumbered by embarrassment, I redoubled my commitment to indulging every urge and scratching every itch. The Gordian Knot of my sexual and cinematic proclivities remained tightly wound, and I could finally give up on any fruitless attempt to unravel it. My nervously clenched fist became an open hand, ready to reach out in search for the increasingly strange titles – in the vein of *Trans-Europ-Express* or *Story of O* – I now count among my most cherished. Now free of my blinders, I could look upon the heretofore forbidden, and I loved what I saw.

I DIDN'T WANT TO BE LAUREN BACALL, I WANTED HER

Izzy Alcott

WHEN I WAS A CHILD, Saturday afternoons were synonymous with glamour. I grew up in a particularly uninspiring, rain-sodden corner of the UK in the 1980s. There was nothing to do at the weekend, nowhere to go, and I was often trapped inside by the incessant mizzling rain that Britain is so well-known for. Even television was a bit of a dead loss as – remember, this being the UK in the '80s – we only had four channels.

However, there was always an old movie showing each Saturday—anything from shadowy film noir to 1950s musicals in lurid Technicolor. With little else to do and an impressionable mind, I ate them up. Sometimes the plots were easy to follow, sometimes I had no idea what was going on. It didn't matter, because I was there for one reason: the beautiful actresses up there on the screen.

There was Grace Kelly; Jayne Mansfield; Sophia Loren. It wasn't just that they were gorgeous; they were sexualised.

Each of them was groomed to perfection, corseted and thrust under a spotlight in their underwear in the guise of vaudeville costume. Due to old censorship laws, sex didn't make an appearance, but the suggestion of it was everywhere: swollen red lips and jiggling hips, saucy winks and lingering kisses. I had no idea what sex was or even what was being hinted at, but I could tell that it was something breathtaking, and I searched for it in my everyday life to try to make sense of it.

I was disappointed. The only women I knew were my teachers, my mum's friends from the Women's Institute and the local shop assistants. They were all growing out their perms and wearing sensible skirts. I barely registered them as women, because to me a woman had soft flesh spilling from a sparkly corset, a tiny waist, glossed lips and possibly a garter. Garters were a fascinating addition. Fat Brenda from the corner shop almost definitely did not wear a garter under her checked nylon housecoat. My mum didn't either: it was all six-packs of gigantic floral knickers from M&S in her underwear drawer. Posing in front of the mirror in my greying vest and knickers with frayed elastic, I decided that I would wear a garter when I was a beautiful grown-up lady. I sucked in my tubby 8-year-old gut and tried to picture myself louche in sequins and furs, with an hourglass figure and winged eyeliner. Admittedly, there was quite a lot of work to be done.

I was a sturdy, plain and unpopular child coexisting uncomfortably with the shiny, pretty girls in my class. They spent break times making up dance routines in the playground and being ordered about by the traditional Alpha Mean Girl—the one who was the prettiest and meanest of the bunch. Whilst they glowed, I squatted, troll-like, in the corner by the drains, poking in the dirt with a stick. I thought dark thoughts and tried to be invisible, but it never worked:

'Did your grandma make your jumper?'

'What's wrong with your hair?'

'Don't look at her, it'll hurt your eyes.'

Whatever. I believed with the unquestioning faith of the evangelist that one day I would show them. It wasn't entirely clear what it was that I was going to show them, but I was pretty sure that it would entail six-inch heels and a swipe of red lipstick.

I quickly worked out that to be accepted, you needed boys to like you. For boys to like you, you had to be beautiful. It was the early '90s, and beauty standards were basically a scrunch perm and a neon shell suit, neither of which I was allowed. But I knew that the secret to true male attraction lay in the Hollywood curves and teetering heels that mesmerised me, so I pored over my mum's old 1950s film annuals and studied the pictures and interviews to work out what I had to do to turn myself into an iconic beauty.

Apparently, a 36-24-36 figure was something to aim for, and luckily for me, my body moulded itself into an hourglass during my teens. I copied make-up from *Gentlemen Prefer Blondes* and I took my style tips from Natalie Wood in Gypsy. I pulled in my waist, pushed out my tits and waited for the men to show up. And after a few false starts and some tough lessons (1. Don't have visible emotions; 2: Never forget to shave your legs; 3. Nobody's dream girl wears a fleece), it worked. I was beautiful and I knew it because men told me that's what I was. As I'd suspected, they loved a bit of old school glamour (or maybe they just really like stockings).

I understood how they felt. Women were hot. Breasts were amazing. The drab women of my childhood were replaced by the perky teenagers that I went to school with and their older sisters. I watched men stare, slack-jawed at their rounded breasts and, well-concealed behind sunglasses, I did the same. I was never quite sure if the feelings that stirred inside me were sexual desire or the exhilarating thrill of the thought that men would look at me like that too.

I digress. So there I was, looking the part. Now the only thing left to do was get good at sex. This wasn't a problem because as a woman it's easy to be good at hetero sex: all you have to do is look enthusiastic and know how to make it look good for you. Men eat that shit up. I did whatever they wanted me to. I even slept with women occasionally. That had fascinated me for a long while and I loved kissing them, touching them and watching them. But sex with women wasn't as important as sex with men, because who cared what women thought of me? It was the male gaze that I sought, and nothing else would do. I saved the girls as a kinky sideshow—just a conversation starter. There were no lesbians in the films that I'd modelled my life upon. In fact, they didn't depict any women caring one way or another about how another female looked. Cinematic women existed only for the male gaze, and therefore so would I. With inspiring titles such as *How to Marry a Millionaire*, it seemed prudent to follow their lead.

Thankfully, you can't stay that much of a dickhead for long and eventually, I got over myself and settled down. In my late 20s, I met and married my best friend—a kind man with an evil sense of humour who shared my love of old films and obscure music. I didn't give a backwards glance to the pretty girl I'd been sleeping with just before he came along. She'd been fun, but now I had the ultimate in fairy-tale movie ending: a man wanted to marry me.

Cue music, roll credits.

We settled in a small town, had a son and eased into cosy domesticity. Wiggle dresses and stockings gave way to stretchy jeans (much more practical with a toddler). But I stuck with the makeup and my collection of big fur-collar film-star coats as a reminder of my life before parenthood. The glamour had faded from my life, but I didn't really mind. I'd ticked all the boxes, I was an accepted member of society and now I could relax. We were happy. I was a little restless, but it felt like enough.

Then one day I met her. She wasn't a movie goddess. You'd never see her on the silver screen. She was quiet, unassuming, self-conscious, and she couldn't meet my eye when I spoke to her. She also had the best arse I had ever seen in my life. She was openly gay, something that didn't register much with me other than to prod memories of my former dalliances with women. I brought out the memories one by one and inspected them. They didn't seem that significant. We became friends, and I recognised in her eyes that she was seeing me in a way that my husband hadn't seen me for years.

For the first time in my life, I did not want to be that actress. I didn't want to be on that pedestal—not for her. I wanted to scrub all my makeup off and offer myself to her as I was. I held out my vulnerability to her like a gift and in return, she showed me hers. She saw me. We saw each other.

I didn't want to cheat on my husband. I agonised over it, thinking that if I could just kiss her once then it would all go away, that the itch would be scratched, that I could put it neatly in a box like I had all the women that I'd been with in the past.

I kissed her. It didn't go away.

When I slept with her for the first time, I knew with startling clarity that I had made an error a long time ago: I was gay. I was a massive lesbian. I hadn't wanted to look like those women in the movies. I had wanted to fuck them.

I went over and over the past in my head, obsessively looking for what I'd missed. I needed to know how I'd screwed up this badly. Here is what I saw:

Six-year-old me gazing, spellbound at Marilyn Monroe, her dress flying up above her head, her thighs exposed. Ten-year-old me ripping the underwear pages out of the Kays catalogue and hiding them in my room to study later. Sixteen-year-old me sitting on my best friend's lap, holding her hand, our foreheads touching as we sang along to the radio and smiled. Eighteen-year-old me reading magazines and skipping past all the pages featuring semi-naked male models giving the readers their best smouldering gazes. Everyone skipped those pages, didn't they? Nobody really fancied male models. We all just pretended to... didn't we? My entire life: never looking at a man with longing, never feeling aroused by their hard bodies as they thrust into me, never thinking of men in terms other than friendship or how to make them want me.

It turns out that it's easy to choose men when men constantly choose you, and I'd made myself into a commodity to be chosen. I had become everything that a man could ever want. Unfortunately, I never gave any thought to what I wanted in the process. But with my head between her thighs, breathing in the scent of her, I knew that this was it. It had always been what I wanted, but I'd been too obsessed with my need for male approval to see.

I sometimes wonder if this is how all femme lesbians are made. Did they also confuse lust for something that they aspired to be? How I look is too much of a part of me for me to change it now. Fortunately, it transpires that some lesbians like curvy women in corsets and suspenders just as much as men do—the only difficult part is getting them to realise that I'm one of them.

I hurt my husband. The sweet man that I married was bewildered when I told him what I was. Had my marriage vows been a lie? Had I known the whole time? I hadn't, I reassured him, and I'd meant every word I'd said on our wedding day. It's no comfort, I know.

I wish I had a sweet coming-out tale, but mine will always be about a woman who ended up being unfaithful to her husband because she swallowed the misogynistic view that women existed for male pleasure. The silver screen shone so brightly that I couldn't see past its outdated notion that women exist for male ownership. I was so caught up in cinematic beauty and the version of life that it pedalled that I failed to see what was under my nose all along.

I'm not sorry for having loved the films that got me into this mess in the first place. I will always smile at Lauren Bacall flirting her way through *The Big Sleep*. I'll always cry when Audrey Hepburn runs through the rain looking for her cat in *Breakfast at Tiffany's*. My heart will always break for

Humphrey Bogart when he puts Ingrid Bergman on the plane at the end of *Casablanca*. I can't apologise for that.

But I wish that somebody had explained to me as a child that real life is not and should not be like that. All it would have taken was for an adult to ask me the right questions: Don't you think it's unfair that the women in these films don't seem to have much personality? Isn't it silly that their happiness depends on being wanted by a man? Don't you think it's appalling that they're treated like objects by men?

Because it was and is appalling. Had I worked out my sexuality earlier, I'd have realised that I was objectifying those women just as much as any man.

This hasn't altered the way that I view the films, although I understand now that the female characters have greater attributes to aspire to than their attractiveness to men: the fierce political loyalty of Ingrid Bergman as Ilsa Lund, for example. Or the playfulness of Audrey Hepburn's Holly Golightly.

Moreover, I don't want to sleep with the beautiful movie sirens even now that I know what I am. As I watch them on screen, I feel that I'm sharing the sofa and a bottle of wine with them as old friends. And when one of them drops a coquettish wink mid-dance routine, I smile back, knowing that we're in on the same joke.

FANTASY AND DANGER

DEATH CULTS AND MATINEE IDOLS
Pamela Hutchinson

ON SUNDAY JULY 21st 1957, a group of London schoolgirls witnessed the death of James Dean in Finchley, a suburb in the north of the city. It didn't matter that Dean had actually died two years earlier on September 30th 1955 in a Porsche Spyder whilst speeding down Highway 466 near Cholame, California. When the teenagers, described as "Teddy Girls" in the *Daily Mail's* report, witnessed one car skidding into eight more at a set of traffic lights they mobbed the two men staggering from the wreckage. Some of them fainted, others screamed: 'It's James Dean!'

'I told them not to be silly, that James Dean was dead,' a man who was driving one of the other cars told the *Daily Mail*, 'but they didn't seem to believe it. It was a fantastic scene.' Although three of the cars had to be towed away, no one was hurt in the accident. For the *Mail*, it was a collision that had no news value beyond the girls' excessive display of emotion and morbid misidentification. The nameless driver claimed he had to drag the girls away from the objects of their attention: Martin Vandervell (cousin of racecar owner Tony Vandervell), who was at the wheel, and his passenger, a Mr John Leyton of Hendon. Leyton was the blond hunk who caused all the fuss, but he wore the burden of being a dead idol's double lightly, telling the *Mail* that he had been mistaken for Dean 'once or twice before.'

This news story was just the latest in a long line of articles in the British papers about not just the death of James Dean, but the wildly emotional, even psychotic behaviour that followed it. It was what the *Mail* called "This Cult of Deanery". Poets and playwrights were touted as the new Dean, who had himself become the posthumous voice of his generation. The obscenities of rock 'n' roll and the delinquencies of youth were blamed on his bad example. Even suicides were explained away as a symptom of Deanery: desperate acts by men and women of all ages who were driven to the brink of insanity by their grief at his death. Who knows exactly what makes someone hurt themselves in the name of a movie actor they have never met, but perhaps it had something to do with the paradox that this brooding youth embodied. Dean himself appeared to be the only one capable of understanding exactly what it was like to experience the pain he caused when he died. The fact of his death made his fans need him all the more.

Dean's death was arguably bigger than his life. Whilst officially there were 600 mourners at Dean's funeral, four times as many fans gathered outside. He died when he was only 24 years old, beautiful and demonstrably talented, yet with only two substantial screen credits to his name as troubled teenage sons in *East of Eden* and *Rebel Without a Cause*. His raw sexiness and ability to portray emotional complexity made him more than simply another handsome young actor. This was a young man you could imagine falling in love with in an instant if he lifted his eyes just a little as he smiled at you. You could imagine getting into trouble with him. No one would ever understand you so completely. No one would be so sincere when he told you that he loved you. That's why you could imagine, too, that if he left you one day, you would never recover. Maybe it was also why every sexy blond man in a speeding car could bring you right back to that moment – the moment you heard that he was gone – his neck snapped by the side of a highway more than 5,000 miles away.

MANY OF THOSE NEWSPAPER ARTICLES had a wry sense of déjà vu. The Dean frenzy was just a repeat, many assumed, of the scenes that accompanied the 1926 death of Italian-born Hollywood star Rudolph Valentino. His was an unglamorous death, due to peritonitis—a painful infection of the stomach lining. Valentino lay sick in a New York hospital for days before finally succumbing to the illness. He was 31 and at the very height of his fame. His career took off in the early 1920s, and he played screen lovers that were physically strong but emotionally troubled. Men openly despised him for being powerfully sexy and masculine on one hand, and confusingly effeminate on the other—with his dapper clothes and gleaming jewellery. His films were known as "homewreckers".

When he died, mourners crammed the streets outside his funeral in New York—as many as 100,000 in some reports. There were stories of women fainting and screaming. Tickets to his latest film, *The Son of the Sheik*, flew out of the box office. For years afterwards, a mysterious woman dressed in black would visit Valentino's grave on the anniversary of his death, to lay a single red rose. Or sometimes several women; Ditra Flame, who claimed to be the original Woman in Black, noted that on several occasions she failed to make her pilgrimage because there were so many women in mourning clothes crowding the graveside. Now that Flame and many of the others are gone, a guide at the Hollywood Forever Cemetery dresses up each year to keep the tradition. Nearly a hundred years later, my friend Lucie takes every August 23rd off work, buys a box of chocolates and watches his movies. That's the date of his death, of course, not his birth.

Back in 1926, some women in particular took the news of Valentino's death especially hard. Agatha Hearn, a mother from New York, shot herself with a sheaf of his photographs clutched in her other hand. I've even read that two girls in Japan leapt into a volcano. In Italy, Mussolini implored young women not to kill themselves but rather to channel their love into motherhood instead.

Peggy Scott, a 27-year-old actress from London, was surrounded by Valentino's photographs when she took the dose of mercury chloride that killed her. The note she left read 'with his death my last bit of courage has flown.' What's particularly grotesque about Scott's death is the inquest that followed. The court, or rather Valentino's associates, seem to have been obsessed with disproving the implication in her note that she knew the actor personally. 'In 1922 Rudolph helped me to carry on,' wrote Scott. 'Please look after Rudolph's pictures. He has helped me over lots of stiles unknowingly.' Friends of Valentino, including one woman who flew in from Los Angeles, testified that Scott could not have met her idol and he was not to be implicated in her death. It all seems horribly unnecessary now. Scott may have been just a fan, but she drew strength from the brooding, handsome heroes Valentino played on screen.

These stories remind me of a theme emerging from the coverage of young women grieving both Dean and Valentino. Critics and commentators fall over themselves to sneer at what they perceive to be an excess of feeling. Almost always, too, you read the cutting line: *these supposedly distraught young women haven't even seen the films.* There's a right and a wrong way to respond to cinema, and this isn't it.

MY GENERATION HAD A JAMES DEAN, and his name was River Phoenix. He was a beautiful, androgynous youth who made his way apparently effortlessly from child actor to teen idol. Like Dean, he was blond and handsome. Like Dean, too, he seemed to have greater depths than other teen idols. Phoenix was a vegan from childhood, did humanitarian work, campaigned for Bill Clinton and exuded a purity that was almost imperious. Here was a guy who wasn't just cool and sexy; he was trying to save the planet as well. He was a guy you didn't just want to chase, but to impress.

When Phoenix died at the age of 23 in the early hours of October 31st 1993, all that changed. Phoenix died at the Viper Room, a Los Angeles nightclub, from what the coroner called 'acute multiple drug intoxication.' He had massive amounts of morphine and cocaine in his blood. Far from being, as he claimed, so squeaky clean he considered a chocolate bar and a can of Coke to be an illicit treat, Phoenix was a habitual recreational drug user. So when teenage girls mourned

Phoenix – and of course we did – we weren't just bereft at losing him, but the ideal of him.

As for me, I moped around in a T-shirt advertising one of the last films he had made, Gus Van Sant's *My Own Private Idaho*. My parents had bought me the T-shirt for Christmas, but I was 12 years old when the 15-rated film about male sex workers was released, so of course I'd never seen it. In proclaiming my devotion, I was borrowing some entirely un-earned hipster cachet. The films I had seen Phoenix in were mostly more wholesome—just like him, I was assured. Maybe I was more devoted to the man in the magazines than on the screen. Is that so wrong? It certainly wasn't cool. My friend Theresa confessed to me that her gran died around the same time as Phoenix and, if only in passing, she thought to herself that it was a 'double-blow.' If lusting after stars is a fantasy we comfort ourselves with, these early deaths teach us that our dream lives can be just as messy and disappointing as reality. Thirteen-year-old Philippa Abbott, who burned a candle for the star, told the *Independent*: 'This is the death of our dream.' In *The Daily Telegraph*, however, there was a familiar taunt. Quentin Letts reported that female sixth-formers in private schools were building shrines and organising special assemblies to mark Phoenix's passing. 'And at Roedean,' he wrote, 'girls were off their doughnuts at tea, pushing away plates with sad shakes of the head. From 14-year-old young madams, there is no stronger expression of grief.'

IN JANUARY 2008, when we considered ourselves to have long since grown out of teenage crushes, Theresa and I were suddenly confronted with our past selves. In a square just a few yards from our office we stumbled into the set of the new Terry Gilliam film. We asked who was in the film, but the men in fluorescent jackets winced. They clearly didn't consider the cast to be that impressive. 'Um, there's Verne Troyer... and Heath Ledger. If you remember who that is?'

Did we? We certainly did. We were far too old to try tracking Ledger down in the streets of London, but were delighted to spend our lunch break reminiscing about how much we loved the hunky Australian actor, especially in *10 Things I Hate About You*, the breezy teen update of *The Taming of the Shrew*, which was by that time nearly a decade old. Ledger plays Patrick, the Petruchio figure, and we thought he was dreamy, not least when he sang "Can't Take My Eyes Off You" to Julia Stiles. When we got back to the office we told our colleagues about our discovery, aware we were regressing a little. *Heath Ledger's new film is shooting just over there!* Most of them weren't impressed.

Ledger probably wasn't at the shoot in London that day, however. And in fact, five days after we stumbled across the set of his final film, *The Imaginarium of Doctor Parnassus*, Ledger was dead. He was 28, the same as us. Like Phoenix, he died of an overdose of drugs—but these were prescription medicines taken in dangerously large amounts. He was discovered unconscious in the afternoon of January 22nd by the housekeeper and died shortly afterwards. It was a horribly lonely death, and he left behind a daughter who wasn't yet three years old. In the city, crowds gathered on the streets outside as the news spread.

The newspaper where I worked, like many others, ran several articles on Ledger, discussing the talent he showed as an actor in Ang Lee's *Brokeback Mountain* and other such serious films. *10 Things* barely got a look-in. And soon his memory would be defined by one of his final performances: not Parnassus, but his leering turn as the Joker in Christopher Nolan's *The Dark Knight*—a cartoon villain in a macho franchise. After all, Ledger was too serious an actor for his memory to be left in the hands of teenage girls.

IS IT HEALTHY TO MOURN so publicly the death of a man you have never met, like the Teddy Girls, the "young madams" and the many Women in Black? It's certainly true that it is helpful for a young person to be acquainted with death before it really hits them. We continue to perform this grief, to practise mourning in a safe space, far away from our real loved ones. Mourning becomes about homage too, rather than loss—a sign of respect for the actor's talent, his always unattainable beauty. I think about all those sneers in the newspapers, and I wonder why male journalists felt the need to belittle this grief. Film criticism, just like filmmaking, is a male-dominated industry—it may be the case that too few of the people writing about movies understand this particular kind of emotional pain. What this public mourning represents is a rare instance of female fans' voices rising to the surface of film discourse. There's something quietly radical about that.

You can make a more cynical argument about our need to grieve when stars die too soon. There's a reason that the quote about living fast, dying young and leaving a good-looking corpse is often misattributed to James Dean. His death itself has a dangerous allure. We look for perfection in our stars: flawless beauty, youth and charisma. We project something more meaningful onto even their most casual gestures. When film stars die young, it's terribly sad—but it also means their mythical perfection remains intact. They're too beautiful to live, and you never have to imagine them growing old. What would have happened to Phoenix had he grown older alongside his buddy Johnny Depp? Would he have made bad films? Bad choices?

WOULDN'T YOU LIKE TO MEET the Teddy Girls who caused a scene at the traffic lights that Sunday in 1957? I would. And it wasn't hard to work out the identity of the handsome blond in the passenger seat. The John Leyton who went on to star in films including *The Great Escape* was only 21 years old at the time of the crash and studying at a drama school nearby. Surely that's the Deanalike in the *Daily Mail.*

It was. Leyton has retired now, but I spoke to his manager, who contacted him on my behalf. The truth is that Leyton was indeed a passenger in a car crash, but the rest is a little bit of a stunt. On the day of the crash, some of the girls who studied with Leyton thought it would be fun to pose for a few photos with him in his wrecked car—trading on his resemblance to Dean and hoping to get a little publicity. Did the readers of the *Daily Mail* believe it? Well, I did, just a little—especially after all the other stories I read about people driven insane by grief over the film star's death. Perhaps we should take those with a pinch of salt also.

Being mistaken for Dean certainly did Leyton a favour, even launching his pop career in the 1960s. Producer Joe Meek remarked on the similarity and had him record a series of rather morbid pop songs. "Johnny Remember Me", a track about the ghost of a young woman haunting her lover, was banned by the BBC for having too many references to death. The record went straight to number one, combining Leyton's twangy vocals, his particular appeal, and a message of grief, desperation and love enduring into the afterlife. It turns out that girls aren't scared of death—not if they have love to guide them over the threshold. Leyton was singing "Johnny Remember Me" on tour well into his seventies, to crowds of women who were all teenage girls once.

I won't ever forget how I felt about River Phoenix back in 1993. Or how the only people who seemed to understand were other teenage girls. What I didn't know then, but I do now, is that this grief connected me, rather than isolated me, from other generations. The women who filled the streets for Valentino, or laid flowers for Dean, are the same as my peers who lit candles for Phoenix and Ledger. So too are we linked to the teenagers who posted about their grief for Paul Walker in 2013, or Anton Yelchin in 2016. Mourning a movie star is a rite of passage, a stile we climb over on the route to adulthood and nothing to be embarrassed about—whatever the men from the newspapers say.

WHAT DOES IT MEAN TO DESIRE AN ONSCREEN ABUSER?
Eloise Ross

TALL, DARK AND HANDSOME. It's a well-worn description for a reason—because for many people this physical form
has a clear appeal. This description is sometimes used as
shorthand for the pinnacle of the desirable masculine form,
includes no reference to character, manner, or personal
ethics. It implies charisma, yes, but it's essentially all about
the look. Often, women are taught to think about a man's
appearance rather than personality, to consider visual status
over behaviour.

This might go some way to explaining my intense desire
for Oliver Reed, the brooding, magnetic film star I first
encountered as the abusive Bill Sikes in Carol Reed's *Oliver!*
(1968). He first appears on screen as a silent shadow, inviting
entwined feelings of fear and desire for his still-absent body.
The build-up to his entry is key; characters have been longing for him to appear and, in effect, the audience also waits
anxiously. In a corner of London hidden within a labyrinth of

cobblestone alleys, a dog scampers out into the dim light and the shadow of a man's torso looms over him on a brick wall. The shadow barely seems as though it's attached to a body at all, but more to a tenebrous spirit, simply a coat and hat floating along and ruling the city's darkness. The torso moves closer, its shadow looms larger and soon his legs become visible—giving his body a greater sense of menace. It's clear a man is there, but he's mysterious, and that mystery suggests intrigue. In terms of cinematic identification, this introduction of the man as a silent shadow lays the groundwork for the art of seduction.

I don't know how many times I watched *Oliver!* as a child, I only know I watched it often. There are three things I recall from all those repeat viewings: I loved Nancy (Shani Wallis), and I hurt every time I saw her beaten to death; I was terrified of the brutality of Bill Sikes (Oliver Reed). Yet, inexplicably, and in conflict with my care for Nancy, I was extremely drawn to Reed as Bill. This contradiction and these conflicting emotions seem to me to be at the heart of cinema. Film has the unique capability to mix both horror and desire – attraction and repulsion – using the platform of fantasy.

But how can personal attraction withstand repulsive behaviour? How could I identify with Nancy as a victim, yet feel a strong desire for her abuser? Did I confuse the cruelty of his snarling expression for sensitivity, vulnerability? I don't think I did. There must be something more powerful in Reed's magnetism. It was his dark eyes, his mutton chops (my weakness) and his laconic sensuality. The overbearing presence of his body and absence manifest in his silence suggests a complex unknown figure, a tease, a holder of power. As a child, I knew he was cruel. As an adult, I understand that although Nancy's expression was, at first, full of adoration, it was later overcome by an acute fear that I can feel deeply from my own experience in the world.

I don't think that I saw tenderness in Bill, nor do I think that I misunderstood him. Perhaps the desire stemmed from fear; everyone with whom we are supposed to identify for the majority of the film has some deeply felt admiration for Bill Sikes. It would be too frightening to challenge this status quo, and so the obvious thing is to follow.

In *Oliver!*, Bill Sikes's name is sung before it is spoken, and spoken before his figure is seen. The boys sing: 'We could be like old Bill Sikes if we pick a pocket or two.' Afterwards, the boys are talking about Bill, and Oliver's (Mark Lester) ears perk up, as though he knows this name belongs to an important figure. Oliver will meet him tomorrow, Fagin (Ron Moody) says. But later that night, Fagin sneaks out and we follow him, along boardwalks through the gritty London streets to a local pub next to a canal. The glistening surface of the water is clearly fanciful for a dirty 19th-century London— but this is a musical, after all. Its escapism is powerful; it beautifies the ugly to make the slums of London fit for the glory of its musical numbers. And that first glimpse of Bill is one worthy of someone on such a pedestal.

Of course, a flesh and blood man follows the shadow. A medium closeup introduces him properly. His stovepipe hat is worn and the frayed collar of his taupe corduroy coat is upturned, framing his face and those famous dark mutton-chops. He doesn't speak, but his blue eyes glisten like the canal beneath the moonlight. After an encounter with Fagin, he continues to walk in silence, greeting his girlfriend Nancy with a nod. After drinking and eating in solitude at the pub and he wanders off, Nancy in tow. His first words are to call his dog, Bullseye, a name that both recalls the perfect execution of a fired gun and echoes the sound of Bill Sikes's own name.

The next time Bill is on screen, he's roused from sleep by Nancy, who is cooking breakfast for him. He growls at her for waking him and although he declares that he loves her, he seems to do so begrudgingly. Although a commanding presence on the London streets, here he is tired and supine, in a position classically framed as vulnerable. It's portrayed as a tender moment of coupledom, and Bill's anger is understandable. He's not mean, he's just tired! What is important here – all the more so when he kills Nancy – is that in his language he is dismissive of Nancy's personhood.

Making note of these moments is key for me, now. None of Bill's other actions in the film are romantic or kind, and he never seems to wish to win the favour of anyone around him. Yet he had it; he had mine. I knew that this figure was a murderer, a domestic abuser, and more generally a bully. It's clear he is unkind to Nancy and that she is manifestly afraid of him long before he kills her. But in paying close attention to him, it strikes me just how unpleasant he is. He does very little in the film until Oliver is taken away and threatens to disrupt their status as hidden thieves, well into its second half. From then on he does more (including an entire sequence where he steals Oliver to break into a rich man's home) that isn't part of my memory of him. Most everything is heightened to a cartoonish – Dickensian – villain status. Despite this, I still desired him. I mostly remembered the sexy parts.

When I was younger, I was aware of the cruelty some men would inflict on women, and that they would do so with some sense of preordained right given them by the hierarchical division of gender. Often, men would leverage this cruelty to encourage a stronger connection, greater subservience, greater fear masked as adoration. I knew that this happened and I was even victim to it, though I didn't realise it at the time. In recent years – and this has been amplified by a more open public discourse about and push against systemic gender-based violence – I have begun to reframe certain experiences I had as a child and teen; to reconsider interactions I had with strangers, with peers and even role models. After speaking with many of my friends, I recognise this process as upsettingly common. It's fascinating to think that, perhaps, I've extended this reflection to Reed in *Oliver!* I can now understand how the narrative, and the language of the cinema, places him on a pedestal.

There's a level of shame for me, as a woman and a feminist, to realise that I may have discarded my own urge for emancipation because I was essentially seduced by a thuggish arsehole. This happens all the time, with power tilted significantly towards "traditional manhood". It would be an impossible endeavour to list all the culprits in this mode, but it includes Marlon Brando in *A Streetcar Named Desire* (1951), Michael Caine in *Alfie* (1966), Bradley Cooper in *A Star Is Born* (2018), maybe even any James Bond. Men so often get to be cruel and yet irrefutably desirable because they're sexy. Of course, there's Barbara Stanwyck in *Double Indemnity* (1944), Ann Savage in *Detour* (1945), Claire Trevor in *Born to Kill* (1947), even Glenn Close in *Fatal Attraction* (1986)—but these are femmes fatales, archetypes inserted into stories to explore a specific type of historical fatalism. When it comes to men, the dangerously sexy attitude is more insidious. It's not in service of a particular genre or mode. These men are everywhere, engaging in repulsive behaviour that we are meant to forgive – even welcome – because we get their sexiness along with it.

Sure, when in the context of a movie I can have fun with a fictional figure at a distance, but such interactions absolutely have had repercussions for my own life. I've never been treated as badly as Nancy was treated by Bill, but there is definitely a related spectrum of harmful behaviour that I have forgiven. In retrospect, I wish I hadn't. It's not as though it's all Bill Sikes's fault, or indeed all Oliver Reed's fault for being so beautiful. The power of cinema is that it can stimulate a desire that transcends the intellectual. By focusing intensely on Reed's eyes, his expression and his gestures, the film invites us to desire him. With this invitation to desire comes an invitation to fantasise about him in a way that ignores any darker qualities. Too often, films don't question the figure of the dangerous, seductive man—they simply present him as deserving of his supremacy.

Cinema doesn't exist in a vacuum; it is the product of the society that creates it, and it comes alive when received by an audience. Films are fantasy—yet they can also indoctrinate us, condition us, and it can take years to have the distance to assess whether something is being condoned or criticised. I know that Bill murdered Nancy, and examining this further, I see that her murder was not the result of a random outburst—it was the endpoint of a relationship defined by an imbalance of power. I always knew that what Bill Sikes was doing was wrong, but the cinematic machinations behind his presentation baited my desire.

I didn't stand up to his unspoken challenge; I fell for him, and I remain conflicted. He's monstrous, but he's so damn sexy. Two things can be true at once.

THE KISS, OR WHAT THE MOVIES NEVER TAUGHT ME ABOUT DESIRE

Jessica Kiang

THE FIRST TIME I KISSED A MAN I was in love with, I thought: *mine.* Just that one word, over and over again—bounding and rebounding, lighting up my electrified insides like a pinball racking up the jackpot: *mine, mine, mine, mine, mine, mine...* It surprised me because everything about love is a surprise. But also it surprised me because it wasn't simply a matter of degree. It was not simply an amplification of a familiar feeling. I had no internal lexicon to describe it.

Every erotic experience of my life to that point could be couched in terms of the romantic notions I had magpied together through the years, notions approximately illustrated by an eclectic stew of movie images and exchanges, some overtly sexual, others not: Grace Kelly switching on all the lamps in James Stewart's apartment; Kathleen Turner in *Body Heat* (1981) watching through half-lidded eyes as William Hurt removes her underwear; Sean Young breathing 'Put your hands on me' to Harrison Ford in *Blade Runner* (a scene recently re-evaluated from the standpoint of consent, which I'm afraid makes little difference to its purchase upon my un-woke libidinous imagination).

But this kiss, the tip of a spike of unprecedentedly hungry desire, existed outside all of that imagery, different not just in intensity, but in type. I was unprepared for such forceful acquisitive instinct and even a little ashamed of my ungovernable, obliterating possessiveness. The thought now occurs to me that in some ridiculous, tightly knotted place inside, it struck me as unfemale, as though in that moment of presumably maximal heterosexual femininity I felt, to the best of my imagination, like a man.

Manohla Dargis wrote a beautiful, gently agonised article for *The New York Times* titled "What the Movies Taught Me About Being a Woman" and her rueful lesson number one is that women are there to be kissed. This quality of "to-be-kissed-ness" echoes the idea, as propounded by film theorist Laura Mulvey (who also coined the mighty useful and consequently mighty overused phrase "male gaze"), of "to-be-looked-at-ness"—a term pointedly hilarious in its ungainliness. The hydra-hyphened contortions of its passive voice draw attention to the difficulties – and the sheer paucity of language – in trying to distil a cinematic expression of womanhood back into women ourselves, of creating an embodied, recognisable, first-person sensation out of a third-person impression. If women have traditionally been objectified in cinema, the term is an attempt at subjectification and, of course, it doesn't quite work. Because what is it to *experience* "to-be-looked-at-ness"? What is it to *feel* "to-be-kissed-ness"? They are attitudes to be struck, games to be played, costumes to be tried on, not states to be lived through or passions to be owned.

With affection and regret, Dargis spools through the forced and coerced kisses of everything from *The Quiet Man* (John Ford, 1952) to *Baby Boom* (Charles Shyer, 1987) to the aforementioned scene from *Blade Runner* (Ridley Scott, 1982). And she describes the 'fog of erotic violence' that is generated between the leads in Samuel Fuller's seedy 1953 spy noir *Pickup on South Street*—a film for which the emblematic image gracing its DVD cover is of star Richard Widmark arched possessively over co-star Jean Peters. One of his hands is cradling her head, but so tightly that you can see the indentations of his fingers on her cheek; the other is gripping her shoulder, tensed and clawlike. Peters' arm is folded against his chest in a gesture of either defensiveness or capitulation—and her tiny smile suggests the latter. She is the perfect image of "to-be-kissed-ness"; he the absolute embodiment of the idea of "mine".

The movies never taught me to think "mine" directly, but I learned a roundabout version of it anyway. I understood the "mine" impulse through the eyes, lusts, lips and fists of male protagonists whose greedy agency over their actions has never been in question—and whose straightforward entitlement to the gratification of their unembarrassed carnal instincts has not, until recently, been substantially challenged. The visual language of romantic conquest and ownership is the province of men, after all, as illustrated by that classic *Pickup on South Street* pose—the man towering proprietorially over the woman made tiny and helpless in his looming shadow.

It is not that onscreen women can never have power in these situations—as the Stanwycks, Crawfords and Davises of the classic era, and the Weavers and Stones and Turners of the late 20th century proved. Indeed, in that little smile and the fractional distance between their faces, even Peters (the second wife of Howard Hughes, trivia fans) retains something of herself despite the engulfing embrace. But as is almost always true even in these more enlightened times, it's a power derived from withholding and here, Peters is about to surrender it. For women, the movies teach us, to be kissed – and all that comes after – is to lose, to be caught, to be vanquished, to be annihilated in the maelstrom of someone else's "mine". One of the great lies that cinema helped foist on the world is the idea that women find blissful fulfilment in this sort of wholesale capitulation and eradication—when in fact our desire can be as greedy and selfish and monolithically covetous as that of any man.

So to suggest I grew up internalising that fallacy – to such a degree that it informed many of my early interactions with the erotic – is to state the blitheringly obvious. Some might ask how a mere few decades of movie storytelling can have a fundamental effect on something as foundational as desire, and the only reply is: how could it not? Especially as the notion of the male gaze (hey, I said the term was overused, not that I wouldn't use it) did not spring to life fully formed from the minds of original filmbros the Lumières in 1895, but was inherited by the cinema from centuries of storytelling prior. Icelandic sagas and Homeric epics, Biblical parables and Greek myths, Shakespearean theatre and penny arcade peep-shows, cowboy serials and blockbuster spectacles have always assumed male consumers. Within those men's lusty, id-driven narratives, the women who show up are almost always there to-be-somethinged: looked-at; rescued; decoded; denuded; mistrusted; relied on; adored; despised; idealised; castigated; won; lost; unzipped by virtue of a magnetic watch; or smooshed in the face with a grapefruit. We are there to have things felt about us, not to feel.

And so it's become my little project to look for the moments in movies when – however briefly – women get to own their desire, to express a simple "mine-ness", with no deeper agenda other than the satisfaction of a voracious urge. It's easier to say what these characters are not than what they are: They're not the vamps who prowl through a haze of cigarette smoke to use sex as part of some manipulative plan, nor the needy good girls who negotiate the terms of their surrender only as long as a stable relationship or marriage is on the table. Nor are they the "cougars" who are, as the term suggests, animalistically proving their alpha status by weaponising their sex appeal. Nor are they the psychos who take possessive desire to such extremes it becomes pathological. This last category is large and most often seen in the form of the erotic thriller, for instance Glenn Close boiling bunnies in *Fatal Attraction* (Adrian Lyne, 1987) or Sharon Stone playing the lusts of the men and women around her for her own sociopathic amusement in *Basic Instinct* (Paul Verhoeven, 1992). But it's also a staple of the arthouse: the increasingly deranged Betty (Béatrice Dalle) in *Betty Blue* (Jean-Jacques Beineix, 1986); the frustrated sadomasochistic Erika (Isabelle Huppert) in *The Piano Teacher* (Michael Haneke, 2001). And it will come as a relief to the many millions of my prospective lovers who are fond of their appendages that – although she is in many ways the logical endpoint of monomaniacal, covetous female desire – I don't regard Eiko Matsuda's erotically obsessed prostitute in *In the Realm of the Senses* (Nagisa Oshima, 1976) as a kindred spirit. Where are the onscreen women who are not made unhinged or ridiculous or weak by the expression of their desires? Who are not repulsed by their desires, but understand them, own them and act on them (or not) for no reason other than that thirst demands slaking?

I have found rare instances, here and there, in strange places. In Maggie Gyllenhaal's lascivious smile as she deliberately encloses a worm in an envelope addressed to her lover/boss in Steven Shainberg's *Secretary* (2002). In *The More the Merrier* (George Stevens, 1943) on the porch when Jean Arthur grabs Joel McCrea's face and kisses him after their long, gorgeously handsy walk home (for my money, the sexiest movie scene of all time—and if you need more convincing, writer Sheila O'Malley has written an unimprovable beat-by-beat dissection of it for her blog *The Sheila Variations*). And though it screws with the template somewhat, I've found it in Angela Bassett's Mace – one of my favourite-ever female characters – who for much of the duration of Kathryn Bigelow's *Strange Days* (1995) is unrequited in her love for Ralph Fiennes's Lenny. But unlike most of cinema's "steadfast best friends who are obviously really The One", Mace never pines and never petitions. Her want of Lenny is entirely her own business. It is hers the way that kiss was *mine*.

The common thread running through these three admittedly random examples is that not one of them is simply an inversion of the traditional model of male desire.

Secretary is about a dominant/submissive relationship that one simply can't imagine working the same way were the genders reversed. The scene from *The More the Merrier* features Arthur prattling away to McCrea about her boring fiancé even as she plays with McCrea's fingers and snuggles into his insistent embrace; a man behaving equivalently would be a cad. The long-suffering Mace exudes a patient, self-contained resolve that is nothing like the ideal of the male romantic hero, who is all about action and intervention. These scenes are not about simplistic substitution—say, a male body being objectified instead of a female. They are not, as I once wrote in a piece about Dakota Johnson's staggeringly regressive sex scenes in the staggeringly inane *Fifty Shades of Grey* (Sam Taylor-Johnson, 2015), about seeing more naked johnson than naked Johnson. Such glib inversions smack of tokenism and, more crucially, perpetuate a way of looking and a mechanics of storytelling that were built by the very system we need to dismantle. Our erotic ideals, so long unserved by the media we consume, have grown into and around existing representations like ivy and are now too tangled up in that history to make such easy reversals an adequate marker of radical progress.

Even if its expression is simple, desire is complex—what it lands on; how it grows. And for women, there's another layer to negotiate because direct, like-for-like association is not the only thing that goes on when the lights go down. Often, we subconsciously ingest ugly, unexamined notions about how to be a woman in the world and how to pantomime a performance of female desire that all but erases one's own erotic agency. But we can also sneak off-road under cover of darkness and relate—not to the woman being owned, but to the man doing the owning. Cinema might be a powerful, masculine-coded master, but women viewers can be disobedient to its demands; we can subvert and co-opt. We have become adept at doing so, at identifying across lines of gender and sexuality. We've had to because historically so little cinema, even that which has been marketed towards us, has ever fully believed in us as the originators of our own perspective.

So I stole from cinema an idea of selfish, conquering desire even if I never felt like I owned it, and that subversive thrill was part of its guilty pleasure, like purloining a Caravaggio from a gallery even if it could then only ever be examined alone, in secret, with all the curtains closed. Covert though it might be, it's a flexibility and an adaptability that women have had to learn that men haven't. It has always been my contention – all due respect to my male colleagues – that it gives women an advantage as critics and, quite possibly, as people, to be fluid in where we can locate ourselves on screen.

If (as a straight woman who's watched a lot of films) my gaze has been queered, it's an offshoot of the patriarchy for which I am grateful—not that any amount of solidarity, adaptability and resilience developed by any oppressed group exonerates the oppression. Still, there is a rigidity of critical development that can occur when everything is made for you, and women – in whose number are of course included gay, bi, trans and other queer-identifying women whose personhood has historically been even less of a consideration to mainstream cinema – have never been bestowed with that gift/curse.

So there are benefits. But there are also complications. The route back to ourselves and to our ownership of our desires is circuitous, like a game of "Whisper Down the Alley" where the message at the end comes out so garbled as to be incoherent. In her brilliant *New Republic* review of Lisa Taddeo's non-fiction book *Three Women*, Josephine Livingstone writes: 'This is one of the toughest betrayals to confront, for a politically conscious woman who dates men: the realisation that your desire for men, which you can do little to alter, is inextricably woven with every other interaction you have had with men, including the bad.' To this, I might add: "including the fictional".

The questions then become: How much time and energy should we expend unpicking the less savoury aspects of our attractions, and how much should we forgive ourselves our problematics and move on? How do we admit that some of our erotic impulses might have their basis in unwholesome, regressive or reactionary arenas, but that they too are valid because they have become part of us? The self-flagellation of women disturbed by the discovery that our cinematic desires have some aspects of internalised misogyny (how could they not?) is itself sexist. It keeps us distracted and shameful, absorbed in self-policing, casting sideways glances at one another's inclinations. We end up in a back-ward-looking, endless unknotting of our kinked-up lusts and thirsts and ideas of hotness. Instead, we could be pushing onwards to a reclaimed cinema in which we can forge new ways of expressing, exploring and celebrating the multifari-ousness of desire.

Film is a place of infinite possibility. Complex though the universe of desire might be – whoever is feeling it, at whomsoever it is directed – everyone should be able to find in the movies the thrill generated by a charged glance or an electric touch, or a kiss beneath an archway that floods your whole being with liquefying joy and the all-conquering sensation of "mine".

FROM FEMALE SUBSERVIENCE TO EATING MEN ALIVE
Sophie Monks Kaufman

HE THOUGHT HE GOT LUCKY, but he got so unlucky. He is Erwan (Nicolas Duvauchelle), a horny teenager in Claire Denis's *Trouble Every Day* who has been watching the house where Coré (played by French sex-symbol Béatrice Dalle) is held captive by her doctor husband Léo (Alex Descas). Erwan doesn't think to wonder why she is locked up. Instinct propels him and a friend to break in when Léo is at work.

Coré has escaped before. As such, the door to her bedroom is broken and she is contained by planks nailed across the doorway. Through these planks, he sees her: white dress, black eyes, juicy mouth. She is waiting for him. He reaches out, entranced. Through the planks they lace hands, stroking each other's fingers. She pushes a finger into his mouth. He sucks and his breathing becomes ragged with desire. Needing closeness, he starts tearing down the planks, baring his teeth with the exertion of separating wood from nail. Once he has made space for a good view, Coré slowly hitches up her dress to reveal that she's not wearing underwear. He rips aside the final plank.

What follows is flooded with contradictory emotions: ecstasy and grief, pleasure and terror, sex and death. The scene starts like a heteronormative male fantasy, with the twist being that Erwan's body is the subject of the camera's gaze. Cinematographer Agnès Godard lingers in extreme closeup on his pale chest, panning across his moles, hair, belly button. Coré is straddling him on top, shrouded in darkness. She kisses him, running her hands all over, and manoeuvres his cock up in between her legs. Tindersticks – a band integral to the films of Claire Denis – gradually begins playing, adding instrument by instrument, until the layers build to a primal throb of melancholic yearning. The music goes full-intensity – powered by all the sorrows of this world – as a lover's lick turns to a cannibal's attack. Moans of pleasure turn to winces of pain. Her teeth clamp onto his chin and he tries to turn away, but she has him. Now he's screaming and sobbing and choking. Skin is ripped from his body. Shrieks curdle the atmosphere. She grins, feeds and continues to ride him. Blood covers her face and body, as she laps at and slaps her dying lover, laughing with abject delight. The sounds are awful.

It's hard to talk about relating to a cannibal without incriminating yourself. Maybe this essay is a concession that I will never run for public office. For the record, I do not crave human flesh. I have not killed and have no immediate plans to kill. The kinship is not literal. When I first saw *Trouble Every Day* at Deptford Cinema it seeped into my bones. I am haunted by Béatrice Dalle and Coré who exist as two sides of the same coin. The former has lived beyond convention. In 2016, she told psychoanalytic French TV show *Le Divan* that, whilst on acid, she broke into a morgue with friends and tasted a corpse's ear. Her energy translates to an unruly screen presence that most directors don't know how to use. Denis – who worships her beauty – is an exception.

Coré is a caged beast made spectacular by the full bloom of her savage desire. Denis styled her with depraved sensuality: black eyes and hair; white skin and dress; blood, so much blood. 'She nearly fainted when she saw Béatrice Dalle emerge on the set of *Trouble Every Day* in her wardrobe and makeup,' according to a profile in *The New Yorker*. 'We had to stop shooting,' Denis recalled. 'I couldn't breathe.'

There is a second cannibal in *Trouble Every Day*: an American male one. Whilst Coré lives in captivity, Shane (Vincent Gallo) is free, beginning the film mid-air with his new, ingénue wife, June (Tricia Vessey). They are flying from New York to their honeymoon destination: Paris. She is oblivious to the fact that he turns into a flesh-eater when horny so will never consummate their marriage. Instead, he feeds on women he deems more disposable.

I have watched *Trouble Every Day* countless times and am no closer to understanding why Denis wrote the male cannibal with enough self-possession to function in society, whereas the female cannibal is a slave to her impulses. Nor am I closer to understanding why sometimes, in the middle of doing something else, I will think of Béatrice Dalle's Coré and want to cry out. My empathy comes from understanding the loneliness that can grip you after an alienating sexual encounter, for her eyes are wet with remorse after each murderous orgasm wears off. She suffers the cumulative despair of one who has to keep throwing another regret into a locked basement in the mind. Léo cleans up after her kills, burying bodies as she waits in the car. Denis finds gallows humour in Dalle's expressive face: hangdog like a naughty child, but instead of having a face smeared in chocolate from a stolen cake her face is smeared with blood.

I am not behaviourally aligned with Coré. I am not dominant; I am closer to submissive, but that term doesn't cut it. Submissive sex is a preference, not something that makes you feel alone during intimacy. Despite being physically confident in the art of seduction whilst clothed, once naked I consider myself so grotesque that I die a thousand times inside. The only way through is to become an object before my partner's desires. I – a great believer in meaningful communication – can't speak for myself. It might seem wild that someone whose mind leaves their body during sex feels an affinity for a character who is violently present, but it leads to a feeling akin to Coré's post-coital despair. Instead of being dejected about the dead body in my wake, I am dejected by my own body—a dead weight. I am wary of my attraction to men out of a realistic fear that if I pursue it to its conclusion, our connection will wither when it should be at its peak.

Yet it doesn't always go that way, and this is what keeps me hopeful about lust. When sufficiently confident, or confidently wasted, sex is what makes me feel the most alive. I have had a smorgasbord of dalliances to optimise the sudden appearance of bravura at odds with my regular operating mode. Earlier this year, a man on a dating site asked about my sexual history. This prompted me, in a long night of the soul, to tot up the number of guys I've slept with. Each time I thought I'd settled on a final figure, in crept another one-night-stand in an excruciating sensory flash. Amongst the good times were guys whose names I don't remember. One had lots of shoes neatly lined up in a white space-pod of a room; another had a hipster moustache that my housemates mocked; another lived in a tent in a warehouse in Hackney Wick. I am not proud of these memories lodged in my psyche like splinters, for most of them do not correlate with satisfying experiences.

The satisfying ones I do not regret.

At my most despairing, I have concluded that the only solution to my particular affliction is to find – then take permanent refuge in – a loving, long-term relationship where cerebral and soulful connections compensate for my inability to lose myself in pleasure. I rose-tint my previous long-term relationship. Even when the sex was not great it was loving, and to be held in love is heaven. My higher brain function is aware that no man can save me from my neuroses but my lizard brain thinks that is absolutely what men are for. However, scaring up a good and reliable man is not so straightforward, and indeed, seems dependent on presenting like a conventionally attractive gal. Arriving at a sanitised feminine ideal is, in its own backwards way, a power move, and yet I am also terrified of the regressive state it runs one aground in. This regressive state is expressed with stark absolutism in the next film I am to discuss.

Bryan Forbes's 1975 TV movie adaptation of Ira Levin's book *The Stepford Wives* has a horror premise that cuts to the chromosomes. In the idyllic Connecticut suburb of Stepford, men are killing women and replacing them with robots that look and sound like them but have no will or desires of their own. These fembots' days are full of cooking, cleaning, gardening, providing sex on tap and, sometimes, malfunctioning. Joanna Eberhart (Katharine Ross), a newcomer to Stepford, thinks there is something suspicious about the servile behaviour of her female neighbours – save for two who have yet to be replaced – but her husband (a villain) gaslights her into believing that she is being irrational.

'I'll just die if I don't get this recipe,' says Carol Van Sant (Nanette Newman) in a softly melodic voice. Her hazel eyes are glazed. She has coiffed brunette hair and is covered up in a floor-length patterned dress which trails across the lawn of her garden party. She is doing the rounds for her guests, stopping at different groups to deliver her line: 'I'll just die if I don't get this recipe.' She repeats it four times before her husband hustles her inside their house. Carol is an important character, being the first fembot the Eberharts meet on arriving in Stepford. She comes over to welcome her new neighbours with a casserole, triggering an early note of discord between Walter (Peter Mastersen) and Joanna. She is creeped out; he is just a creep. Shortly afterwards Walter will tell Ted Van Sant: 'She cooks as good as she looks, Ted!'

What makes *The Stepford Wives* terrifying is there is no leap between the sci-fi horror premise and its real-world application. 'You want me to disrupt our lives for the second time in a couple of months for some fixation you have,' scoffs Walter to Joanna. They are fighting because Joanna's best friend Bobbie (Paula Prentiss) has changed from a snarky, Stepford-suspicious woman who wears trousers and crop tops to a glazed, dress-wearing automaton with a suddenly less-sophisticated vocabulary. Another symptom of transformation is that Bobbie's previously chaotic house is now pristine. 'When are things going to start sparkling around here?' yells Walter at Joanna, refusing to engage with the dehumanisation that has taken place with their friend. When female independence – heck, a female pulse – is dismissed in exasperation, the underlying thesis is that it doesn't matter if a woman is truly alive. Want to exist as more than a domesticated, man-pleasing robot? How naïve. This is Stepford, baby, where your insides mean nothing. Worse than nothing. Your insides are an inconvenience.

In a pivotal scene, Joanna stabs a fembot, screaming: 'I bleed. Do you bleed?' This formerly vivacious woman, now an obedient simulacrum, gently reprimands Joanna on a loop: 'How could you do a thing like that? How could you do a thing like that? How could you do a thing like that?'

And yet... for all the muted tragedy of the Stepford wives, there is a sedated security in submission. When you don't pose a threat to the controllers of the status quo, you blend in, slip under the radar, escape violent attention. You can't kill someone who's already dead inside. If you grow up aware of your own strangeness, afraid of the constant shadow of alienation, then a place on the master's arm at least scans as a recognisable social position. I was in my early 20s, crawling out of my skin with physical self-loathing and temping at a law firm when the 50-something-year-old partner casually referred to me as "a pretty blond". I had passed! A powerful man recognised me as appropriately decorative! Inside, I rejoiced. The rush of superficial acceptance is intoxicating before you've figured out the value of your depths. This episode still haunts me because I have not fully outgrown my susceptibility to male approval. I straighten my curly hair to appear sleeker; wear clothes that emphasise my breast-to-waist ratio; sport heels that lengthen my legs. When, inevitably, I am catcalled in the streets I think: I walked straight into this. I might as well have created my personal dress sense from the playbook of "How To Indulge The Male Gaze".

The contradiction of beauty is that I inhale pleasure that I look good, and exhale paranoia because I look good. The smaller animal seeking a mate must still remain alert for predators. I don't believe that all men are rapists. Some are beautiful companions that enrich the road ahead. I want to find those men, date them, know them and love them, yet when one first appears it is in Schrödinger's body; inside that male form could be what I want, or it could be an agent of destruction.

Neither *Trouble Every Day* nor *The Stepford Wives* end well for their heroines. Both are strangled; Joanna with a dressing-gown cord by her fembot alter-ego. Coré by fellow cannibal Shane, who then leaves her corpse to blacken in a burning building.

Shane gets to stay alive and free. He resists the urge to have sex with his wife and instead sates his appetite by raping and eating a hotel chambermaid—without consequence. Why do men and their desires get to run wild?

'Because we can,' says the Head of the Men's Association when Joanna asks why he is turning women into fembots. 'See, think of it the other way around. Wouldn't you like some perfect stud waiting on you around the house? Praising you, servicing you, whispering how your sagging flesh was beautiful no matter how you looked? Think of it the other way around.'

No.

The frankly miraculous properties of good sex come from its sheer improbability. When all the necessary elements align I feel like I am going to pass out in paroxysms of astonishment. What I want – an emotional connection, physical attraction, a progressive understanding of gender relations, a hint of traditionally masculine dominance – I have learned that I want through a process of trial and error. I have had dispiriting and degrading experiences that I am none too thrilled to remember. Even so, they have instilled an appreciation for intimacy and a sense of the vitality of articulating the true strangeness of one's personal sexual journey. The presumption tends to be that if you've had a lot of sex, then you've enjoyed a lot of sex. I've endured a lot of sex. There is a special type of pity reserved for women who struggle to enjoy what should be the apex of pleasure. Those who have an easier ride to sexual liberation are sad and surprised to hear it.

But why be surprised when this is a patriarchy and messages are still pumped out about placing a man's peccadillos ahead of one's own? In Stepford, Bobbie and Joanna overhear a hot wife having afternoon sex with her dowdy chemist husband, performatively moaning, 'Oh you're the best, Frank,' before flat-out screaming 'OH, YOU'RE THE BEST. YOU'RE THE KING, FRANK. YOU'RE THE CHAMPION, FRANK.' She is not really feeling that good. Robots do not experience sexual pleasure, but she has been programmed to make affirmative sounds to placate the ego of the man who let her human version die.

'I want to die,' says Coré to Léo 33 minutes into the film, as he uses a yellow sponge to dab blood off her naked body. She is pliant, like a well-behaved child at bathtime, turning over when he needs to sponge her back. This is when she whispers: 'I don't want to wait any more. I want to die.' Her horny cannibalism is a pathology that will only intensify. Denis frames her leading lady like a tragic force of nature. When hungry, she has no memory of the downsides to being a maneater. She is governed by the supernova intensity of each passing moment. She is out of range of moral teachings, but still connected to her conscience.

To me, she is extremity itself, a symbol for our most antisocial sexual tendencies, whatever they may be. She is a creature cut loose from time in the sense that time is a continuum of associated events over which we have some agency. Coré is irretrievably lost in the present; more vivid than anyone else and more dangerous.

Maybe the trick is to recognise what compulsion your inner Coré represents and to navigate around her as painstakingly as you would the Men's Association of Stepford.

OUR BODIES,
OUR SELVES

DRY
Willow Maclay

WHEN I THINK OF SEX AND DESIRE, the image that comes to my mind is of chastity belts. We all know that chastity belts were used in the past to preserve virginity and control the bodies of women, but my conception of chastity is a little different. For me, a chastity belt isn't a metaphor for chasteness, but an image of gender dysphoria. You can't unlock something that isn't there. My perception of myself and the reality of my flesh are at odds with one another. My mind doesn't know what to do with my useless body, stuck between mixed biological realities with no real answer to the question: why can't I be like her?

I was born intersex. I have XX chromosomes, an underdeveloped uterus and an underdeveloped penis. None of these parts of my body works, but my brain perceives itself as female. My body is overrun with hormones for a few days every month and I'm met with cramps, bloating, mood swings and migraine headaches, but unlike cisgender women, there's never blood because there's nothing to pass. I'll never become pregnant. My doctor says this is 'all the nuts and bolts of PMS, without any of the actual payoffs.'

I wish I could do these things to their fullness instead of living in the half-truths of cisgender womanhood, but that is not a realistic wish, and I won't see the question of my body solved in my lifetime. I'm stuck in between worlds—not quite a cis woman, not quite a trans woman. An alien inside my own skin. A woman nonetheless, but something half-formed. How do you form your own desire when your body is beyond any common definition of what people find attractive in a woman?

What's more, where does that leave with me with sex as someone who wants to have vaginal intercourse, whose desires are tied up in things like procreation and giving away my own vulnerability to a man? How can I emphasise any of these things if I'm locked out of my own body and more often than not ashamed of my own form? The answer is complicated and, in the context of cinema, something resembling my own experiences is nearly nonexistent. Cinema has historically had little space for minority persons, and that's even truer when it comes to things like sex. In the movies, a man is more likely to vomit than to come when seeing a body that looks like mine, and I internalise that feeling. Who wouldn't? I didn't pick my body, it just is—but cinema has said, with resounding clarity, that someone like me isn't capable of sex, let alone love. A body is just a shell. It isn't good or bad, but when you're told over and over again that your flesh is poison, it's hard not to buy into the propaganda.

I lust over men as many women do, but I'm left out in the cold when the question of sex comes up. Sexual intercourse for a body like mine isn't sustainable in cinema. Stories where Idris Elba, Chris Evans or Michael B. Jordan are soft, caring and lustful over a body like mine don't exist, because society at large doesn't find me attractive when my clothes come off. If I'm dressed, I'm just another woman, but my flesh tells a different story. I'm a riddle to men and, often, a puzzle box to myself. My hips cascade like a falling wave, but when the tide washes out there's this abstraction, a negation that renders everything else a lie. I'm a girl until I'm not, and that turns me into something monstrous. Cinematically, this leaves me only one option for identification: with things that aren't human.

Historically, transgender women have been presented on screen in one of three ways. The first and the most prevalent of these is in the "trap" narrative, which is when a straight man goes to bed with a transgender woman he previously assumed was cisgender and reacts with disgust or violence. This is most famously represented in *The Crying Game* (1992), which saw its main character vomit at the sight of a penis on the woman he thought he was in love with. He later does realise that she's more than her body, but that isn't the prevailing cultural image from the film. The damage had already been done. It was considered a great twist, instead of the horrifying reality for straight trans women that it actually was. Popular movies and television shows such as *Ace Ventura: Pet Detective* (1994), *Austin Powers: The Spy Who Shagged Me* (1999), *Family Guy* and *The Hangover Part II* (2011) all copied the scene note for note but emphasised that this was actually hilarious.

The second of these common cinematic depictions is tied into castration anxiety, whose first seeds were planted all the way back with the work of Alfred Hitchcock. *Stage Fright*

(1950) and *Psycho* (1960) both have late-act reveals which show gender-variant people to be no more than murderers. Later, these characters were incorrectly interpreted as transgender women. Brian De Palma put his twist on it in 1980's *Dressed to Kill*, which features a real-life interview with transgender woman Nancy Hunt taken from an episode of *The Phil Donahue Show* and reconfigured to put a face to the madness that is men wearing dresses who say they are women. This antiquated trope still exists today with films as recently as James Wan's *Insidious: Chapter 2* (2013) using the trope of the monstrous feminine to prop up his villains.

The third option is finding representation through synthetic bodies, robotics and science fiction. For me, this is where I find characters whose bodies and minds function like I do, specifically in their inability to grasp what isn't there and not understanding why they are made differently. The crown jewel in this case, as it pertains to my own desire as a woman, is Jonathan Glazer's science-fiction masterpiece *Under the Skin* (2013).

The film follows an alien creature (Scarlett Johansson) who adopts the image of a human woman on a mission to lure men to their deaths for some unknown purpose. On a surface level, this is about predator/prey dynamics, and the plotting of the film has nothing to do with trans women. But then, the narrative is secondary to the main intention of the film: someone trying to become a human woman in spite of being neither of those things.

Later in the film, the alien begins to reckon with her place in the world as someone that appears to be a woman. She meets a man (Michael Moreland) and they develop a caring relationship. She's quiet and seemingly fragile but is realising both the potential for her humanity and the limitations of her own body (she cannot eat food, for example).

For the first time, she also seems to have some love for her new body. It doesn't have to be a tool anymore. Bathed in amber light, she approaches a mirror and tilts her head. Mica Levi's otherwise haunting score rises and swells for the first time in the movie, underlining this moment as a positive one. There's sun in the middle of a film whose previous palette was made up of the murky greys of Scotland and the black void of Glazer's surrealist touches. This is an acceptance of what she has become and who she is, made all the more powerful by what is lost in the following scene. Everything falls apart when she tries to have sex.

She's lying on her back and the camera is framed with a moderate bird's-eye view so we see her entire body on the bed. The room is lit in that same golden amber as in the previous scene. He removes her jeans and she's staring up at him lovingly. They kiss; the camera moves to a closeup and she stares into his eyes. She wants this moment to be perfect. It could very well be the realisation of her womanhood and her humanity. There's a cut back to the bird's-eye view that shows the man removing his pants enough to penetrate her, but before he does that there's a cut back to a close-up. Mica Levi's score becomes more fractured among the hiss and buzz as there is building chaos and we see the man struggle to enter her. He stares at her and reshuffles his position but there's no entry to be found. She pushes him off of her, startled that it isn't working. She grabs a bedside lamp and pulls it close to her genitals. The music stops. She dejectedly throws the lamp to the floor.

All the joy that was previously in her face is absent. She's framed in dark shadows, the glowing amber gone. The music has vanished. Just the silent hum of her own thoughts. Her eyes are wide open with a flushed look that can only read as sorrow. She can't have sex the way she wants. She spends the rest of the movie as a recluse, barricading herself in the soft hollow of the empty Scottish woods. She can't be human, but it wasn't foolish that she tried.

I'm lying flat on my back and having sex in a dark room only lit by a bedside lamp, with my legs clamped together as tightly as possible. I have on flesh-coloured underwear and I'm tucked, as always. If you blur the image, you'd call my body normal; if you open your eyes fully you'd see that it isn't. If only I could live in that blurred in-between instead of my own stark reality. I try not to think about what everything below my waist is telling me. I bury it deep within my mind and focus on my husband kissing my breasts, a natural part of me, but during all of this I am not giving my body away. I am keeping it hidden. I am juggling pleasure and the bubbling torment of my body's reality. I'm trying to keep the latter dim enough to say tonight was pleasurable, but in a fraction of a second I consciously realise what I'm doing and I capsize. Good try, but your body is what it is. She can't have sex the way she wants.

The question of my own desire is compromised because I know the endgame of my own fantasy isn't happening. The desire to have a normal, functional, female relationship with sex isn't given to girls whose bodies are chastity belts.

In cinema, *Under the Skin* is the closest any movie has ever come to placing a finger on the pulse of my greatest anxieties and experiences of sex. But it is in the work of transgender filmmakers Lily and Lana Wachowski where I find the light at the end of the tunnel. Their debut feature, *Bound*, is overrun with sexuality and visual imagery which focuses on wetness and the placement of hands. It is strikingly observed in a lesbian context, where hands are key. When Corky (Gina Gershon) meets Violet (Jennifer Tilly) for the first time she fixes her kitchen sink, and they emphasise the image of Corky's hands gripping and turning a pipe until water bursts forth, dousing her. It's a metaphor for foreplay that is later capitalised upon when those same hands, still wet, grasp at Violet's heavy cleavage. These characters have immediate sexual chemistry and waste no time getting to know each other; they recognise a good thing when they see it. The Wachowskis had the good sense to imply with wet visual imagery that this was coming. It makes everything breathtakingly sexy, and the amazing thing is that this was directed by two closeted transgender women. They knew what they wanted to do with such precision that one can only imagine they'd been thinking about making this movie their entire lives.

The fundamental fact about transgender women is that we typically know what we want when it comes to our own bodies and sex. Yet we are more often than not shot down by the limitations of our own bodies or failings of the system—with options such as surgery far out of reach due to cost, and an insurance industry not taking us seriously. In my case, I dream about the potential world opened up to me after I fix my body with vaginoplasty. My greatest desire is to be capable of being the woman I know myself to be in every facet of my life. At that point, my sexual desires are going to change, because I won't have to think about what's wrong.

I'll be able to welcome the openness and freedom of knowing that I'm about to get exactly what I want without the burden of my own body getting in the way. My relationship with cinema will likely change for the better too. After vaginoplasty, I hope to fade into the banality of dreaming about Channing Tatum without reservation—or a nagging thought about my own alien flesh. I can be his and he can be mine. We could have soft evenings on couches built for two, underneath blankets meant for one, in a living room filled with the scent of a lavender candle. He'd laugh at my crass humour and call me "babe" in that jock-with-a-heart-of-gold voice he has, and we'd live a perfect life that is only ours. That's what fantasies are about right?

Maybe I can just be me. That's my actual fantasy.

SEXUALITY ROLE MODELS

Raechel Anne Jolie

IN 1992'S WAYNE'S WORLD, we are first introduced to Cassandra Wong as she is playing guitar and belting out vocals onstage with her band, Crucial Taunt. Yet as soon as our protagonist, Wayne Campbell, claps eyes on her, the band's music fades out and "Dream Weaver" takes its place, encouraging the audience to join Wayne in falling in love at first sight with this stunning singer. I did fall in love along with Wayne, but not in the same way. For me, Cassandra was less an instant object of sexual desire and more an instant role model. I was in awe of her commanding presence on stage, of her too-short white denim shorts and her tiny denim vest. I was hypnotised by her effect on Wayne that seemed to stem not from weakness but from power. She was both sexy and strong and taught me, even at eight years old, what it meant to be desirable.

Trips to the movies continued to have this pedagogical effect on me. The films became teachers of sexuality, the women onscreen purveyors of effective flirtation techniques and models of sensuality. At times they were mirrors to my own developing relationship to desire; other times they were aspirational, setting a precedent for what I dreamed of some-day becoming. Unlike *Wayne's World*, which was directed by a woman, not all of these films had the same powerful representations and, in fact, many were solidly misogynistic. These days, I practise what media theorist Stuart Hall would describe as "negotiated readings" of cinema—taking what works and leaving (and usually very loudly critiquing) the rest, or reshaping the narrative to fit my own (as many queer people, people of colour and disabled people are forced to do in a world that too often skips telling stories like theirs/ours). As a young girl, I intuitively had some of the tools to practise that kind of engagement, but admittedly, I was informed by many male-gaze-driven views of women, and so my role models were as troubling as they were saviours. Suffice it to say, the development of my sexuality is complicated.

I grew up in a rural, working-class, predominantly white town outside Cleveland, Ohio. My dad drove stock cars and my mom served cocktails at the local Brown Derby. The first four years of my life were filled with what you'd expect of "white trash" (a label I wear today with reclaimed pride): old cars, messy houses, beer-drinking men and the women who loved them. Then my dad was hit by a drunk driver and, suddenly, life looked very different. I spent more time with my well-educated and culturally refined grandparents, and we eventually moved to a neighbouring town that was still blue collar, but not quite as unapologetically.

The movies were always an escape for me, especially with the tumult of my childhood. At the time, I looked disdainfully on my thrift store clothes and food-stamp-bought groceries, but I can see now that what I was drawn to most in film were stories about women who were just like the ones I grew up with. Excessive. Indecorous. Over the top. Sometimes downright slutty. And, admittedly, usually a little "crazy".

The "crazy woman" trope is employed by movies in ways that have had a serious impact on the state of gender roles in our culture. For instance, consider descriptions of Hillary Clinton during either of her presidential campaigns. Women are seen as unstable, an idea that is exacerbated by pop culture. Furthermore, this notion of "crazy" has created a stigma that haunts people living with mental illness. Yet for better or worse, I found out-of-her-mind women in the movies to be intimately relatable.

Crazy, broken, seductive women were all over early '90s films; I vividly remember Drew Barrymore in *Poison Ivy* seducing a man twice her age. Angelina Jolie practically built her career by playing damaged, sexy women in movies such as *Gia* and *Playing by Heart*. See Winona Ryder in anything, but especially *Welcome Home, Roxy Carmichael*, in which she played a mentally unstable teen (Dinky Bossetti) who misguidedly believes her birth mother is a celebrity. I felt empathy for all of them. I was particularly drawn to the combination of Dinky's weird behaviour (she tries to barbwire her bedroom), androgynous grunge aesthetic (oversized flannels and messy hair), and deep desire (and ultimate desirability). I also connected with the way she placed so much hope in the story she created for herself—if her birth mother really was a famous actress, she could find her and be saved from the struggle of small-town life. I knew that kind of longing. For Gerald (played by '90s

119

heartthrob Thomas Wilson Brown); for her mom; for a way out of a hard life.

I think I knew, even before desire made sense to me, that I wanted to be sexy—and I think I knew, even before I really knew why, that I was damaged. Or at least that I'd be perceived as damaged. And so these stories of broken women finding their way (and leaving wreckage in their wake) were entirely aspirational.

I'm not saying these were ideal role models, but they were all, in their own way, notably powerful. Or at least deeply agentic. None of these women were making choices for anyone else. They were driven by their pleasure, their desire, their passion. And they usually got men to behave how they wanted, even if the repercussions were grim.

Not every character had a tragic ending, though. In addition to the aforementioned Cassandra (presented as stable and brilliant, in contrast to Wayne's eccentricity), there were women such as Doralee Rhodes, Dolly Parton's character in *9 to 5*. Doralee was a perfect blend of totally hot and militantly feminist. She bears the brunt of harassment from both her sexist boss and her sceptical women co-workers, yet remains resilient. By the end of the film, she's won over the women of the office and becomes the ringleader (and lasso-roper) in the kidnapping of her boss to hold him accountable for his harassment. I was mesmerised by her ability to be both overtly sexy and incredibly strong willed. I wanted to be as desired as Doralee was by her colleagues—and as capable of refusing unwanted advances and protesting unjust working conditions (ideally, like Doralee, with the stabby ends of acrylic nails).

Similarly, Cher's Loretta Castorini in *Moonstruck* exerts immense agency over her life, particularly when she decides to follow her desire towards Nicholas Cage's Ronny and away from Johnny (Danny Aiello). Despite having a desire to be taken care of (like any good working-class girl, she at least considers marriage as a method of obtaining economic stability), Loretta knew how to call the shots. She gets her dad to stop having an affair and Ronny (who wants her desperately) to stop moping. Loretta's relationships with men drive her growth more than it does theirs. And rather than being a quirky, meek, beret-wearing coquette, Loretta is a big-haired, high-heeled loudmouth. I could say the same for Cher's character in *Mermaids*, Rachel, who at one point after her daughter (Winona Ryder again) tells her she looks like a 'woman about to go forth and sin' responds: 'Oh good. Exactly the look I was hoping for.' Rachel, like Loretta, knows exactly what she's doing.

So these were my blueprints: wild and misbehaving women who reminded me of the wild misbehaviour I grew up around. They'd continue to serve me as I got older and had real-life crushes (and strategies for getting those crushes to crush back). It's tough, though, for a middle-school or high-school-age girl to truly embody what she wants to embody. There are layers of insecurity, a lack of experience and, for some of us, layers of trauma. But those images were there, tucked away, ready for me to pick from my toolbox when I was ready.

What surprised me was that I utilised these performances of desirability most when I fell in love with a woman for the first time. I had seduced men using some of the coy devices of femininity I'd learned from my idols, but it wasn't until a handsome-as-fuck butch lesbian nervously flirted with me at a college activist group meeting that I was able to dive into the realms of excessive femininity I'd been shaped by. In other words, my first queer romance connected the dots of my class and my sexuality in one profound term: femme.

"Femme", as an identity, has its roots in working-class gay history. Gay bars in the '40s and '50s were the domain of working-class men and women who needed working-class jobs to support themselves and their families. As John D'Emilio explains in his canonical essay "Capitalism and Gay Identity", the industrialisation that forced agrarian family units apart enabled a previously impossible kind of individual autonomy that allowed working men and women to explore same-sex socialisation. Gay bars have been archived as places of escape for low-income queers, as was particularly notable in the case of New York City's Stonewall Inn, considered the home of the modern gay liberation movement. The police violence that escalated at Stonewall was a result of the cops cracking down on queer people, sure—but also poor people.

As for me, my '90s "white trash" roots, combined with my love of the movies and my budding queer romance, turned me into a version of Marisa Tomei in *My Cousin Vinny* (think leopard print, big hair, high heels no matter the time of day or destination; also an immense knowledge of cars). I loved being excessively feminine, "extra" in the best way possible and doing it, first and foremost, for myself, but also... for butch women. There is a lot of debate in feminist circles about whether we can ever truly be resistant to the male gaze when it's so all-consuming—but I'm less interested in determining if it's possible and more interested in exploring what it means to try anyway. What might it mean to continue to honour the calls of our truest gender expression even if it does sometimes pass as normatively sexy? Is there anything more subversive than being exactly who you want to be? Can our high heels be a middle finger to the patriarchy rather than a submission to it? Yes, I think so. And thus, queer femmes keep trying every day. Isn't that a victory in itself?

The characters from the '90s that taught me weren't written to cater to queer femmes, but I found a home in them anyway. Even today, in my mid-30s, I still look to these characters for inspiration. My favourite outfit is a pair of too-short cut-off jeans shorts and a black and red flannel tied at the waist, topped off with a pair of combat boots. It's a hot look; it's a trashy look; it's a queer look; it's a look that turns heads (of many genders). And it's a look I learned from the movies.

'It's good to want things,' Dinky Bossetti says to Gerald after he expresses a desire to kiss her ('so bad') in *Welcome Home, Roxy Carmichael*. Indeed. It's also good to be wanted. I have the women of '90s movies to thank for knowing that.

THE BLOODY SHEET
So Mayer

I CAN TRACE ALL my issues with desire, with cinema and possibly with life to a single moment; a single word.

Yentl.

Yes, I'm blaming Barbra Streisand.

And my parents, who made me watch *Yentl*, which Streisand directed and in which she plays the title role, when I was eight or nine. And my deeply Catholic year eight Religious Studies teacher who made the class watch the film. That was our entire unit on Judaism. She proceeded to direct all questions to me, as the only conservative Jew in the class.

The ones I remember were about the sheet.

That bloody sheet—literally, if you remember the film. The sheet on which Anshel (that is, Yentl-in-male-disguise-as-her-own-dead-brother-so-she-can-study-at-yeshiva) and sweetly naïve Hadass do not consummate their marriage. The sheet with the red wine spilt on it to look like blood, so that Anshel can continue to pass as male rather than risk revealing himself in an intimate clinch.

Questions: Is it real? Do they (meaning: me) really have to do that? Check for blood?

Answer: I don't know.

Answer: I'm too embarrassed to talk about it.

Answer: I don't care. That's not what I'm thinking about.

I don't know what I'm thinking about, or I can't say. I'm twelve and I've just started to realise – really realise – I'm not like the girls at my school. I don't swoon over New Kids on the Block or Tom Cruise, a fact that causes one classmate to throw a cup of ice at me. I'm not interested in getting off with boys in bow ties at bar mitzvahs.

I'm 12 and I'm starting to think that, in fact, I might want to get off with Hadass, played by the lovely Amy Irving. Five years after *Yentl*, she redefined romantic Jewish womanhood in her starring role as Isabelle Grossman, the protagonist of my mum's (and to my knowledge, every mum's) favourite film, *Crossing Delancey*.

It's a kosher romcom: whatever the *treyf* temptations, bookish Isabelle won't let down her Bubbe (grandmother) and marry out, but will come around to the matchmaker's choice: pickle shop owner/Dustin Hoffman-lookalike Sam.

Like Disney's Belle who turns to books to find more than her provincial life and finds her prince under a rough exterior, Isabelle is a vexed feminist heroine. *Crossing Delancy* is triple F-rated, written by Susan Sandler and directed by Joan Micklin Silver, but the ending – much like the ending of *Yentl* – rankles. I think I might want to rescue Isabelle from marrying Sam the Pickle Man; from having to marry at all.

I can't articulate it yet (I'm still working on it now) but I might want to be Anton, the hot goyish writer who offers Isabelle a way out of the Lower East Side. Anton, but less of an asshole.

Like I might want to be Yentl. But I don't want to have to give up being Anshel. And I don't want to give up either being married to Hadass or crushing on her ex-fiancé (and naked swimmer) Avigdor, played by Mandy Patinkin.

At 12, I don't yet have the mental gymnastics skills known as "queering", which will come to enable me to edit every film and TV show I watch so that I can both recognise myself on screen and find an answering form of my desires. I don't yet have words like "queer-baiting" for how mainstream media consistently short-changes LGBTQI+ viewers watching to see characters, relationships and desires they recognise.

Think J. K. Rowling claiming Dumbledore is gay but not actually writing that into the *Harry Potter* books: queer-baiting. This creates an endless cycle: queer-baiting tempts readers and viewers into queering, searching for those hints and clues that there might be a character just like us—which leads to disappointment and demands for more. Rinse and repeat.

Now, we have other screens we use to engage with cinema and TV. We don't just watch any more (the letters pages of fan magazines show that we never did), we interact. We pick up the sheet to see what's beneath; to ask as well as fantasise. To engage when we are enraged. To articulate, together with others who might be like us, or might just like us.

I don't have social media or a search engine when I'm 12 and in that classroom. What I have is: shame. The sheet with the (not-)bloodstain. The blood rushing to my cheeks as my classmates ask me: is that how you (will) do it? And I hear: your sexuality and your gender identity (I also didn't know either of those words) mean you'll need it. Weirdo.

I DID NEED IT, the sheet. In the sense that that's what the cinema screen became to me: a way of protecting myself and a tool for passing as a non-weirdo. As a teenager, I treated everything I watched the way the hatchling treats every animal it encounters in the classic picture book *Are You My Mother?*

Watching *Point Break*, the first 18-rated film I snuck into, I was asking Keanu Reeves and Patrick Swayze 'Are you my desire?' (and if so, is that because you desire each other?) and only secretly whispering it to Lori Petty. Maybe unconsciously what really excited me was how Petty and Reeves seemed like mirror images of each other: dark-haired, big-eyed, thrust-jawed, toned-butt reflections between whom gender blurred.

As Juliet Jacques points out in her memoir *Trans*, the 1990s were a decade in which trans and genderqueer characters briefly became visible as themselves in independent cinema, notably in *The Crying Game*—and rarer still, in films where the character's gender identity was neither a plot twist nor the cause of the tragedy. *Priscilla, Queen of the Desert* stands out for Jacques, and for me. I vividly remember seeing it at the Prince Charles Cinema in central London with my soon-to-be girlfriend, where the film was preceded by a live drag show.

It seemed like cinema had come a long way, making more space for me and my desires (and even desirability) on screen. Even so, the gap remained: between watching New

Queerness flourish on screen and being able to live it in London's Jewish suburbs. So I took my mum to see *Go Fish*, the first lesbian film I can remember ever hearing of – let alone seeing – as an attempt at coming out. She fell asleep, as she had done when we watched *The Crying Game* on TV. With unerring timing, she woke up three-quarters of the way into *Go Fish*, during the sex montage, said 'Pierced nipples!' and fell back asleep. Getting a divorce and becoming the single parent of four children is tiring. But still. You can guess when she woke up during *The Crying Game* and what she said. And the discussion it took us decades more to have.

What I have, at 16, is shame. And frustration: at where I come from and how to keep up with how the world is changing. I watch the films of the New Queer Cinema and want to be part of it; to disappear into it. *I'm a lesbian!* I think, watching *Go Fish* and *Bound* (with the volume on low so my mum can't walk in and fall asleep). I have a word for it!

I'm. I'm.

I tape Western-with-a-twist *The Ballad of Little Jo* off the TV and watch it over and over. I tell myself I'm reconnecting to my childhood when my grandmother babysat me through the medium of Clint Eastwood films (the more violent the better). But now it's the era of *Unforgiven* (directed by Eastwood) and *Bad Girls* (think *Showgirls* with guns); Westerns-with-women are a thing, all of a sudden.

But is Jo, played by Suzy Amis, a woman? Like Anshel/ Yentl, she dresses as a man to survive and thrive in a hostile environment. S/he dresses as a man for the rest of his/her – their? – life. I don't yet have access to the term non-binary or genderqueer. I'm not sure either strictly fits Jo, because s/he's being Jo in the 19th century—when sex/gender and sexuality are commonly understood as being facets of each other, if they're thought about at all.

The viewer knows Jo was not assigned male at birth, but the folk of the frontier town don't, although they suspect that s/he and Tinman Wong are lovers (they are). Jo's secret lasts until death; until the town doctor performs an autopsy. The white sheet is folded over his body. Her body. Their body.

Mine? I don't have the words.

IT'S MY FIRST YEAR at university and I am walking out of the cinema with my best friend, sobbing and sobbing and sobbing and sobbing, but I can't say why.

We've just seen an accidental double bill of *Chasing Amy* and what was supposed to be John Waters' *Pink Flamingos*, but which due to a fuckup somewhere is instead a preview of a Belgian film called *Ma Vie en Rose*.

At the climax of the film, the protagonist – primary schooler Ludovic – is suicidal. Her parents have punished her for both her gender identity (she wants to lose her Y and have two Xs) and her desire to marry Jérôme, her father's boss's son. So she runs away and climbs into a roadside billboard advertising her favourite TV show: the magical, Barbie-like *Le Monde du Pam*. Entering *Pam's* candy-pink wonderland, she pulls her unsupportive, socially anxious, distraught mother Hanna after her. 'Boy or girl, you will always be my child,' Hanna says when she and Ludo return.

Is Hanna's acceptance as much a fantasy as *Le Monde du Pam*? When the family moves to a new town after her father's boss fires him, Ludo has to return to dressing like a boy.

Over the next few weeks, the inarticulate sobbing dissipates into irritation at my fellow students asking me – the only out lesbian in our year – about that scene in *Chasing Amy*: Do they (hand gesture)? Is that how you (head wiggle)? That fucking scene. Where Alyssa explains fisting to Holden, with a coy hand gesture. No one in the film seems to know the word "bisexual".

So maybe now the New Queer Cinema is over? And I'm still waiting for the right words, the right images, the right stories. It wasn't just over between Holden and Alyssa as they went their separate ways at the end of *Chasing Amy*. As I leave the cinema, it feels like something is over for New Queer Cinema's plural possibilities and polymorphous perversions as well. Once again, I don't know where to look for, or at, myself.

I try not to think about Ludo going through the screen, disappearing into the billboard—and I try not to think about her having to return.

I'm 20 and still racked by shame. In my second year, I go alone to see *Kissed*, bunking off a class. It's screening for one afternoon only because the British Board of Classification slapped an X on it for references to necrophilia. It's the first time I've seen a film that doesn't present alternative sexuality as transgressive at best—or gross and liable to get you murdered at worst.

I'm not endorsing necrophilia; I am committed to consent. It's not my kink, but I recognised something in it as perhaps an allegory, or maybe in the title of the short story *Kissed* is based on, Barbara Gowdy's "We So Seldom Look on Love".

Mortuary assistant Sandra (played by Molly Parker in an unforgettable debut) lifts up the white sheet and she looks on love. She looks with love, with compassion and desire at bodies that others find disgusting; beyond the pale; mere objects.

At a body whose desire is frozen, inarticulate and impossible.

I lie under the sheet waiting for her to find me.

I'M STILL LEARNING how it might look if I unfroze and looked back.

In fact, I learn that from books: not erotica, or not exactly. I had a girlfriend who liked to masturbate as she read heavy German philosophy (also not my kink).

But I had worked out that I find more that turns me on in books than in a cinema that has long seemed to discount me. A particular turn-on is the work of critical writers who turned film – and particularly classical Hollywood cinema – into an explanation for what was wrong with the picture. They helped explain why all those curtains closing on a kiss left me cold, and even in a cold rage.

The most famous is Laura Mulvey, whose 1975 essay "Visual Pleasure and Narrative Cinema" was itself written in a cold rage about endemic violence against women offscreen. It remains the most-cited essay in the humanities and (perhaps more notably) the punchline to a joke in *Parks and Recreation*.

Mulvey's essay asks two simple questions about desire: Whose bodies are desirable on screen? And whose bodies get to desire them, on screen and in the audience? She coined the phrases "to-be-looked-at-ness" and "the male gaze" to describe the answers to those two questions as being divided, precisely, by binary gender. Or as John Berger put it three years earlier in *Ways of Seeing*: 'Men look and women appear. Men look at women. Women watch themselves being looked at.'

Berger could express it in simple, direct language. The theorists I found myself reading avidly were facing a more difficult task, the same task I had been facing – secretly and silently – since I was a child. Finding the words for it. For things like the slippage between those two categories of men and women, for the ways that looks might go in different directions.

In the late 1970s and early 1980s, lesbian critics challenged Mulvey, asking: Where do we stand in your equation? What are we looking at, and how? Those are the questions that run through the books I seized (and still seize) with such desire. Books called things like *Queer Looks; How Do I Look; Deviant Eyes, Deviant Bodies*; and (more recently) *Film Bodies* and *Shimmering Images* pose, often in language they're making up as they go along, the very question I'd started asking as a hatchling: Are you my desire? Am I desirable as this? Is this how I do it?

None of them have chapters on *Yentl*, so I still don't know how to think about it.

THE FACT IS THAT TALKING about desire and cinema, for me, requires an entire library, several imagined dictionaries and possibly a different reality. What I mean when I say I'm blaming *Yentl* for this is really that I'm holding my conservative religious upbringing responsible for the shame attached to gender and sexuality; to the body; to curiosity. I went into the screen to get away from all that—and, like Ludo in *Ma Vie en Rose*, I keep having to return to reality.

It's a reality where shame, frustration, exploitation, violence and invisibility are all that's on offer, not just within conservative faith environments but beyond them. After all, it wasn't conservative Jews but a Conservative government who passed Section 28 banning the promotion of homosexuality, just as I was heading to secondary school and ready to learn all about it.

The reality is that the reality has barely changed, despite the articulate loveliness of social media. Or certain parts of it. Tumblr was, for one utopian moment, a venue for so much hopeful, informative, collective discussion of the nuances of gender and sexuality on screen. Then again, so had chat rooms been in the mid-90s when I was still too young to access them.

Those bright spots – moments where the sheet turns translucent (as when Yentl transgressively lifts her father's prayer shawl to the light) and we glimpse the possibility of desire – are still rare. The white sheet (and mainstream cinema remains as white as it does heterosexual, cisgendered and binary gendered) takes up most of the space, both blanking out and covering over anything that challenges it.

'WHO IS STRONG?' asks Yentl's father in an early scene. 'He who controls his passions,' is the answer, a quotation from the rabbinical commentary on the Pentateuch called the Mishnah, which Yentl knows—although she yells it passionately, uncontrollably.

It's this supposed patriarchal wisdom that Yentl will end up exemplifying: she returns to presenting as Yentl (whereas in the original short story by Isaac Bashevis Singer, s/he remains Anshel and heads off to study elsewhere) and gives up her (bi)sexual desires.

After 20 years of writing professionally about film, I find myself wondering if my passion for cinema was a way of controlling my more frightening, difficult passions; those that Yentl, too, gives up. I'm hoping that if I stop going into the screen, hoping to find a way to be (different) (than I am), I might be able to come out the other side.

I might be able to let go of the sheet, of the shame of it; the shame stained on it. To be bisexual, queer, nonbinary, and other words for myself that I will find in future. To be in tune with the ending of *Kissed*, when Sarah McLachlan sings that she's not frightened anymore; she won't fear love.

TRAP DOORS AND OTHER MEANS OF ESCAPE

Amy V. Blakemore

DO YOU REMEMBER THE SCENE in *Aladdin* when Princess Jasmine, a Disney Princess, feeds the villain Jafar an apple? Her body is wrapped in a red negligee, one that tightens around the smallest parts of her body and billows outwards, as if its only job was to delineate her most desirable symmetries. In her seemingly boneless hand, she offers her captor an impossibly shiny red apple and, eating it, he spits a pale hunk of flesh on her cheek. She wipes it away with disgust, her gold chains protesting on her arms and we know, already, that she will have to seduce him to escape. Even if we barely understand the word "seduce" as children, girls like me learn, perhaps for the first time, that our bodies are tools for our own desires. We learn that our bodies are trap doors and, if we are bold enough to open them, we can exit the stage and tell a new story.

This is not what *Aladdin* tells us, of course. *Aladdin* tells us that captors are villains with captives who do not consent.

It tells us that sex is a means to an end as opposed to an end. Thankfully, though, it also tells us that damsels are not always in distress. Princess Jasmine was my first makeshift educator of kink before I knew "kink" meant anything other than an impressive knot, a difficult thing to undo. She hadn't enjoyed being imprisoned, but alone in my room, I did. I wrapped my Catholic School tights around my body; I looked at my reflection and imagined a master who had ordered me to dress this way. Like many women, and like many queer women, I had started building a narrative of my pleasure—even if at the time, I only thought I was playing pretend. Submissive was the term I was looking for, but I wouldn't find it for years, much I wouldn't find "brat", or "breath play", or "impact play".

That's the thing about the movies: they never gave me language, but they did give me a look, a visual fantasy—something I could try on and disrupt with my own meaning. For my long-unarticulated desires, watching the movies became like attempting an escape. They showed me the trap door and I fell into the dark, feeling the walls for an exit. It took me years to realise I would have to build one myself.

My film education made one thing clear: wanting to be seen was dangerous; wanting to be pleasured was whorish unless that pleasure was defined as a deep kiss under a full moon. What does it mean that one of our most glorified kisses in cinematic history happens when the woman is asleep? It means we value "romance" over consent, yes. But it also means that we assume that a woman's desires are dormant—or, put another way, only women with dormant desires get to be princesses.

My second makeshift educator of kink was Alfred Hitchcock's *Rear Window*. In college, in a basement classroom, I first see a wheelchair-bound L. B. Jeffries appear on the screen just as his neighbours appear in their windows: I watch him watch them. The film not only relies on voyeurism to function, it contends that film is voyeuristic, and I sit low in my desk wondering if it will teach me not only about the pleasures of seeing but the pleasure in being seen.

At 21, my penchant for exhibitionism has started to show, even if I don't know how to embrace it yet. Even if the kinkiest things I have done are asking my partner to choke me, asking my partner to spank me, and getting drunk at a house party before having a supremely misguided threesome in which I lose both my friends and my shoes.

On the screen: Miss Torso, as Jeffries calls her—a dancer who, in her apartment, bends and kicks and spins to accomplish even the most mundane of tasks. She bends all the way over, rear in the air, as she gets a snack from the fridge; she lifts her leg up on the counter as she cooks. She must be performing for someone, we think—she must fancy her open window an opened stage curtain.

For the length of the film, I wait for the moment when Jeffries finds her at the end of his binoculars and she looks back: when her eyes flick up and I can pretend they are mine, setting men on fire in their living rooms. And I wait. But the only person who disrupts Jeffries's one-way gaze is a large man in glasses, a murderer, and his furious recognition of being watched becomes the climax of the story. Miss Torso still dances in her window. She is not performing because she is hoping to be seen; she is simply performing. The lights come on and I sink in my chair.

Rear Window taught me that women are ideal objects to be seen, but there is no room for them to delight in that seeing. For a movie that relies on voyeurism to function, exhibitionism is suspiciously absent. I try to make it present. As I get dressed, I leave my windows open—I let my towel drop and look out into the world, wondering if I will hook an eye in the dark of a window, pull out something live and squirming. *Somebody will see you,* my boyfriend says, and the most self-aware thing I can say is: *so what?* How could I articulate that I finally wasn't ashamed of my body, the body I had starved and serrated and demeaned? Fast forward, years later. In the corner of a hole-in-the-wall-restaurant, a man will tell me that my anorexic history has to have something to do with my kinks—with pushing my body to its limits, with enacting a secret hatred for myself. No, I tell him, you are missing one key difference. I never chose anorexia. But I can choose my pleasure. (This is what I wanted to tell him, at least.)

Someday, in Dallas, I will flirt with a woman with perfectly drawn cat eyes as my boyfriend rides on a mechanical bull. We make a bet on his performance, the terms of which I don't remember, but the outcome of which is us kissing. We end up kissing. That night, for the first time, I will be fucked simultaneously: with his cock and with her eyes. She will place her hand on the small of my back and move me up and down. I will wake up glowing: somebody had seen me. And I had seen them back. I had opened the window.

This is how I learned about kink: in pieces, projecting my own desires onto storylines fraught with objectified women, damsels in distress and a non-consensual gaze. My sexual memory of film comes in flashes. *Clash of the Titans*: the equally beautiful Perseus and Princess Andromeda, the way I wanted to be both chained to the rocks and holding Medusa's sheared head. *Ghostbusters*: Sigourney Weaver opening the door in her shimmering, one-shouldered, liquid fire dress and asking 'Are you the Keymaster?' as the wind blows in her hair, her possession made erotic. An unknown title: one night, as a child, my parents tell me they are having a living room "date night" and watching television shows that will give me nightmares. I sneak down because I'm curious, of course. I peer in and see a dead woman in a lace dress. She's splayed out on a velvet couch and a woman in black is standing over her, her lips juicy red, a crooked smile on her face just adjacent to happiness. There is something in her expression that I mistake for desire, though my few stolen minutes make clear that she is the murderer. (Queerness came in snippets, too.)

And then: *The Little Death*, an Australian film from 2014. When I found out that there was a movie that dealt specifically with fetishes – cataloguing them with a title and definition before each narrative arc – I thought I might finally see myself as something other than a victim or a deviant. I thought I might find some language for my desires. I was out of college and in a relationship with a man who I had courted with homemade videos of me fucking myself; a man who knew I was bisexual and had not asked, as others had, if I secretly wanted to have a dick; a man who was particularly skilled at wrapping his hands around my throat and letting go when I tapped twice on his arm.

The movie begins with a man sucking his giggling wife's toes in the brightest, cleanest modern home I have ever seen and I thought: *I might see a couple who is kinky and happy.*

I might see us. There is a woman who is turned on by her partner's crying (dacryphilia); a man and wife who experiment with slipping on different personas (roleplay); and, of course, the often alluded to but rarely depicted rape fantasy, a desire I would later hear others in the kink community call consensual non-consent. But every kink in *The Little Death* ultimately results in a disaster of varying magnitude: a lost dog; an ended partnership; a husband in the emergency room with a neck brace and black eyes; a fatal car accident. Its filmic capacity for imagining the painful outcomes of non-traditional sex is almost comedic. Almost, but only if you are not someone like me, pricked with the hope of representation and then mocked.

Picture this. A wife asks her husband to rape her. He doesn't understand; he thinks she wants him to rate her, to give her a number of a scale of one to ten. *No, rape,* she says, explaining that it's a common fantasy. He attacks her as she's bringing home groceries; it doesn't work because she smells his cologne. She kisses him and thanks him for trying. Then: he plans trickery in a parking garage. They'll be accosted by two men; he'll get "knocked out"; he'll secretly put on the other man's mask; he'll finally take her how she wants to be taken. But he should have known that the trickery is too real; his wife breaks his nose and fractures his neck. The husband doesn't remember a thing. *Did I rape you,* he asks, hopefully, a pitiful circle of his face peering out from his bandages. *Yeah,* she says, smiling, before he proposes to her. *Yeah.* There it is: her desire, submerged, and we already know from the way that she sighs and smiles that tired smile. This is the end of her articulating her fantasies. The end of a brief-lived foray into kink. As the credits roll, I swear I can see her, ring on, rubbing herself hard to the thought of violence that's not violence as she watches the bedroom doorknob, making sure it doesn't turn. At least he tried, she will tell herself. That's what the film wants us to tell ourselves, too.

Perhaps I shouldn't be so hard on *The Little Death*. Forgive me: I am tired of stories that end with an unsatisfied woman and a satisfied male ego. I tell my partner I want him to take me and I tell him exactly how. I am not sure who taught me how to do this, but it wasn't the movies.

The problem really isn't *The Little Death*, or *Rear Window*, or *Aladdin*. The problem is that so few movies explicitly deal with kink, so what we have to work with is kink as salacious, relationship-ruining, all-consuming, non-consensual, pathological—or (predominantly) shrouded. Yet somehow we make the most of them. I buy lingerie like the murdering woman in the unknown late-night feature. I buy a lot of pleather because I think this must be what being kinky looks like. I'm not entirely wrong, but when I show up to the New England Fetish Flea, there are also people in jeans, T-shirts and button-downs. A woman wears a red bodysuit and I think of Princess Jasmine and smile. She is leading two men on leashes and I stop, watching in total admiration. That is not my kink, but for the first time, I am privy to witnessing someone else's. I'm not just seeing it flicker on the screen, not just seeing it lurk in the background like a question, or a ghost. It's a miracle I found these people. Maybe the movies were like breadcrumbs: never enough to satisfy me, but definitely enough to lead me somewhere else.

Scene: I am wearing my pleather skirt and my knee-high boots and a black top and no bra and I sit down in a chair in a crowded ballroom where vendors have set up their wares.

Imagine the sexiest flea market possible, full of wooden paddles with Bibles at the end, wands that spark purple electricity on your skin and leave a delicious trail of burn, custom corsets with boning so strong that your lover can lift you up by the waist and rig you to intricate ropes and hooks (I try one on).

I sit down in the chair for a demo. Why not? It's taken me so long to get here. A man wearing a leather vest straps two adhesive electric pads to the insides of my thighs in front of an impromptu audience. I part my legs and he cordially says *a little wider* as he places the pads on the edges of my underwear, on that eyelid-thin strip of skin, before asking me how intense I want it to be. *Let's see how it goes,* I say, and he flips a switch on a little black box. The stickers begin vibrating and an electric current travels up to my belly button and down to my knees, just barely circumventing my clit in a close hit of pleasure so murderous I could scream. I slouch deeper in the chair, hoping for the electricity to hit that spot in the middle of me, that tiny, brutal button that I always reach for first when masturbating, that tiny, vulnerable button that I was taught to be afraid of. I can't wait any longer. He should turn it up higher, I gesture with my thumb, poking towards the ceiling because I'm having trouble speaking; the pulsing on my thighs turns to a red hot heat, rolling in waves, and now I really am screaming.

When I finally come, I don't say a thing even though everyone is watching. I want this one to be mine—to be a secret written in my notebook at recess, to be a phone call I indulgently ignore, to be a sapphire fishing lure in the bottom of my belly. I want it to be something beautiful I swallowed so no one else can have it. Here I was, being seen and feeling safe instead of dangerous. Here I was, feeling my hands along the wall and finding it. A latch—the way out.

THE FEMALE
GAZE

AVERAGE ENGLISH MEN
Violet Lucca

BEING A FILM CRITIC isn't an entirely respectable profession. In *Hitchhiker's Guide to the Galaxy* terms, I'd probably be loaded onto that second arc along with the telephone disinfectors. Even as far more essential aspects of life fall apart – democracy, the environment – I'm always trying to improve my writing (something I have actual agency over) by strengthening my prose and expanding my knowledge of the medium. I also follow some basic rules to ensure a certain level of editorial quality and respect for filmmakers: not checking my phone during the film; not tweeting about the movie immediately after leaving the theatre; not watching a movie at home on double speed with the subtitles on so I can get through it faster. In a similar vein, I don't write about myself when writing about a movie—I think it's bad form to put yourself before the art, which (regardless of its quality) the writer and/or director have worked on for at least a year to realise.

After all, there's certainly no shortage of bad personal essays online about what a particular movie means to a writer in which the memoir eclipses any discussion (or even description) of the film and ends on a mouse fart of an "and this is what I learned" sentence. That isn't to say that it isn't possible to write something edifying and excellent about art through the lens of your own experience, just that it's very, very difficult to do it well—and the man who popularised this surface-level autobiographical aesthetic engagement (Roger Ebert, the man who replaced Pauline Kael as America's most famous film critic) has legions of uncurious acolytes. Throughout his career, Ebert was also alternately leering and moralising – though often both at the same time – another reason why he never meant much to me. Responding to the brazen horniness that's still practised by a few male reviewers by rhapsodising about Jason Momoa's luscious beefyness in an *Aquaman* review isn't going to create parity, or right some historical wrong.

But all that being said: I may not write about it, but I notice. I mean, have you ever seen Jack O'Connell in '71, where he plays a Brit squaddie lost in Belfast during the Troubles? Even though looks like every other white guy I knew growing up, he's so... erotically imposing. Jamie Bell was distracting in *Film Stars Don't Die in Liverpool*, even though his face is kind of whatever (apologies to Annette Benning). Who would've guessed that little Billy Elliot would've grown up to be such a muscular honey? And Tom Hardy, an unwoke bae who exudes a not-always charming dumbness, helped me get through *Star Trek Nemesis*.

I realise that my attraction to these just-sort-of-okay looking men is largely (well, entirely) due to their accent—

even though I feel the reasons English accents are considered the gold standard of pronunciation are foolery. Numerous studies conducted over multiple decades have shown that people within the English-speaking world associate Received Pronunciation with wealth and higher intelligence (Spanish-accented English usually ranks at the bottom). Some of this privileging is due to the clarity of words ("but-tah" versus the Americanised "buddur"), but a lot of it has to do with media and socialisation. To Americans, English accents are associated with royalty, stately homes where all sorts of romantic misadventures occur, surrealist sketch comedy and tuxedo-wearing spies—supposedly erudite pleasures that the Beeb and the UK tourism industry profit from.

That familiar difference of Englishness remains appealing to me but was once so important that I was willing to build my life, not just my masturbatory fantasies, around it. In my senior year of high school, I applied to Oxford University, a process that involved a lengthy online application, an interview in New York City and a proctored test that I think took about 90 minutes. During those years, I was preoccupied with five things: music, film, dicking around on the internet, spending time with my friends and holding sway over how people saw me. I had previously been a studious, quiet and overweight kid that was constantly bullied—but after dying my hair black the summer before freshman year, I embraced being a fat goth with gusto. I wore voluminous black clothes to hide those parts of myself I'd been taught to hate and directed attention to whatever my sassy Hot Topic tee said. Rather than people telling me I was a "hippo" in gym class, I became more feared (and more respected) than before—after all, this was back when American social panic centred around "secretly satanic" pop musicians like Marilyn Manson and video games. Along with this newfound Machiavellian dress sense, I started exploring other identities and rarefied things that other people didn't know.

Before high school, I had been content to be into anime and British comedies that ran late at night on PBS but as I grew older, I needed increasingly complicated things to make me "different". I was always treated differently, but now I wanted to define that difference myself. I had always been mocked for not being like other girls, and I only saw proof in my flabby limbs, broad shoulders and large stomach, so I chose to embrace the belief that I was somehow "not like other girls". What made me different, then, could never be boys—though, unlike the other girls, I was good friends with many dudes. My dissatisfaction with my body (and hatred of being touched anywhere near my waist) led me to become essentially asexual, sacrificing all sexual pleasure and thought so I wouldn't have to be reminded of my physique. In years since, I have heard many women (in restaurants, in bars, in private) express similar feelings; patriarchy makes us wish we were mist—visible but undefined; present but not too intrusive; gently floating on the periphery.

But I wanted to have some control. And one of the ways I thought I could have control was to go to a place where I would be kind of exotic, and everyone around me would be exotic too. I would be far away from my schizophrenic mother and her well-meaning but smothering antisocial family who had raised me when she was institutionalised. I could rewrite who I was, surrounded by the English, and get a world-class education in the process. But, and perhaps unsurprisingly, I was rejected from Oxford. (Going to public schools in Cedar

Rapids, Iowa in no way prepared me for it.) The worst part was telling teachers and friends that I hadn't gotten in. After telling my Advanced Placement Comparative Government class about my crumbled dream, I went home and replayed the looks on their faces over and over in my head. I cried and cried and cried. And then I couldn't stop crying when listening to "Thirty-Three" by the Smashing Pumpkins so, at my request, my aunt took me to the emergency room. We waited a very long time, and the nurse didn't give me a tranquilliser as I had hoped. My aunt was annoyed, and she told me that I'd better not turn out like my mother. I had to live with my greatest disappointment rather than medicate it away.

Now, I can barely conjure what I had fantasised about my life at Oxford. I went to the University of Iowa, which took me about 15 minutes to apply to, and engaged in the process of rewriting myself without the benefit of rounded vowels. I was only 45 minutes away from home—but it turned out to be a world away. I slowly lost weight and became someone who was perhaps a bit bigger than a woman ought to be, but definitely within the realms of the socially acceptable. I stopped wearing black lipstick. I still cried a lot because I felt like I was a failure. I began to study film instead of the science and psychology topics that I felt I was supposed to study, and came to bond with others about how much we loved it. I even showed up early to class just so I could talk with people. Our discussions about film weren't like the embarrassing, out-of-touch critics who appeared on TV with their thumbs and punny props; we bonded, overstating everything we ever liked or hated about a movie or a director. My desire for film, for connection through film, and the legitimate pleasure I got from those connections, eventually won out over my self-distrust and I realised that I didn't need a "back-up" career. Film wasn't a frivolous thing; it could be my life.

I learned the sensual nature of sharing something with a roomful of strangers in the dark. I started to feel a little less disconnected from my body. Still nursing fantasies of expatriating myself to the UK despite Tony Blair's abominable participation in the Iraq War, I went to London for the spring break of my freshman year in college. (My father, who had divorced my mother and disappeared when I was three, found my number by Googling my name when I was 17. He offered to pay for a ticket to anywhere I wanted – within reason – but not to give me any walking-around money.) I ate cheap baguettes and lost my virginity to a "proper cockney" named Louis Petit (don't worry, it was just a name—he was about average). I sipped a glass of white wine as I watched Bernardo Bertolucci's *The Dreamers*, appreciating the sexiness; I didn't get most of the references.

I returned to Iowa City with a newfound sense of satisfaction. I had realised my dream of touching foreign soil; of being an American abroad; of souvenir sex. I felt as if I had passed from outsider to someone who was slightly more "in". I began living my life, rather than simply waiting for it to start on some imaginary terms; not being allowed to do something by my aunt; being told by thinner, richer, more normal girls that I couldn't participate because of how I looked. I stopped feeling like I needed to Not Be Like the Other Girls and, over the years, I have joined them. Maybe it was a triumph, or maybe it was an attempt to put some very painful things behind me by pretending that they never happened. I'm still mulling it over.

From time to time, I will revisit a film that I loved during that sad, angry, solitary time of high school and be pleasantly surprised I still enjoy it. (I feel as though I've been many different people since then and realise that no, that's not just a "me thing".) Yet when I watch *A Clockwork Orange* now, I'm struck by the pulsating sexuality of Malcolm McDowell's performance, something I completely missed on my first 500 viewings. Sure, it's a really smart, high-modernist fable about personal freedoms that features a confident, clever, archly comic, sadistic and muscular antihero. But there's also the fact that he's so goddamned hot. And he's naked or nearly naked in a lot of key scenes. (Stanley Kubrick, who under-stood the value of living in England and allegedly had an IQ of 200, doesn't get nearly enough praise for really knowing how to shoot a man's body.) When I put on an episode of *The Young Ones* whilst I'm cooking or need a pick-me-up, I breathe in Rik Mayall's cuteness between laughter. Even the sternness of a season one Arnold Rimmer on *Red Dwarf* was once a clit-tickler for young me.

That British sternness is inconsistently erotic to me, and it still surprises me when it strikes, such as when Cousin Matthew from *Downton Abbey* tells his new valet that he doesn't want to BE DRESSED UP LIKE A LITTLE DOLL! Dan Stevens, with his icy blue eyes and floppy blond hair, is an outlier—as he has an overall eroticism (and conventional attractiveness) that makes my thighs cramp up, which strikes even when he's doing an American accent. I didn't watch *The Guest* right away so I could enjoy that poster where he's all beefed up and looking vaguely menacing and imagine my own movie. A snarling Richard Burton and Peter O'Toole would be more classical examples; their pronunciation is just as excellent.

But lest this turn into a rambling list of home county honeys that turn me on (shoutout to the etiolated beauty of Tom Hiddleston) or regrets, I have found that, as much as the media landscape has changed, mediocre English men remain the jewel in the crown of American female horniness. Despite an ever-widening array of TV shows, video games, non-threatening K-pop bands, and the Instagram accounts of bears and Persian muscle men to make them wet, I can still find common ground with almost anyone about, say, how Tom Hardy is pretty sexy. In some ways, this attraction makes it the UGG boots of sex appeal—it's basic as hell but very comfortable.

This sounds like a value judgment, as if this is all just guilty pleasure territory—but it isn't, as there's nothing to apologise for here. The desire to be an individual, something so ingrained in American culture – the need to be The One, as every action movie preaches – is in desperate need of revision. I spent the first two decades of my life so desperately running away from "being like the other girls," but now I recognise that what I pursued was, in fact, largely what everyone else liked. (Sure, I was the only girl on my freshman year dorm floor who didn't have their heart melted by *Love Actually*, but I was getting my English romance fix in less obvious places.) As I have grown older (and arguably more basic), I have come to find the aspects of films that are hidden in plain sight to be among the most challenging and pleasurable things to write about. "Basic" is an abstruse pejorative category that's forever shifting, used to describe things that are so ubiquitous, boring and devoid of personality that they negate the self. Yet what is or isn't basic is more often than not defined by who likes them rather than what they are—so a sense of self is involved. It's only self-deprecatingly applied to oneself or pejoratively assigned by someone else. But things that are "basic" or the "all the same" are still worth talking about, for they create meaning and pleasure in our lives, albeit differently from something that's universally considered "good". Sharing an experience with an erstwhile stranger – either together in a theatre or later in a conversation about a film or TV show or a favourite English actor – is what makes this popular art form so great. To quote a great fictional Englishwoman: 'Only connect!'

DANCE BOY DANCE
Anna Bogutskaya

I.

GENE KELLY was the first man I remember being aware of. As in, I was aware of his body, his movement, his presence. I remember watching him in *Anchors Aweigh*, dancing with an animated mouse (Jerry of *Tom and Jerry*), which blew my little mind in a time before I understood special effects. He seemed huge and light at the same time. He wore short sleeves and tight white trousers.

Who the hell was this man?

In retrospect, having rewatched *Anchors Aweigh* and many other Kelly performances, I've been able to put them into context. I've found better words to articulate exactly what it was that scene provoked in me.

It wasn't just the dancing. Or the short sleeves.

As I sat down to write this essay and re-immersed myself in the sea of YouTube clips and 50p DVDs rescued from CeX shops, I tried to remember those initial impressions. There were the innocent ones—and the filthy ones that followed.

What is it about Gene Kelly that still provokes palpitations? What is it about men dancing on screen that instantly captivates me? Where can I find living examples of men like this? Who are Kelly's spiritual heirs?

As I went back and revisited all the dancing men that have populated my screens and whose movements have stuck in my mind, for reasons both aesthetic and thirsty, I tried to piece together why these men appealed and not others.

II.

WHO ARE THESE films for? They're for lustful women.

Gene Kelly in *Summer Stock* trying to get a newspaper off his shoe. Channing Tatum in *Magic Mike XXL* welding in his workshop, all casual-like. Mikhail Baryshnikov in *White Nights* stretching as Gregory Hines does some crunches on a piano (as you do). Donald Glover in *Magic Mike XXL* walking down the stairs in a bowler hat (just because). Sam Rockwell lighting a cigarette, grooving to Marvin Gaye in *Charlie's Angels*.

These are moments for us to enjoy.

They're not about the men dancing, they're about letting us watch them—and fantasising about them.

There's the canary yellow v-neck shirt that Gene Kelly rocks in *Summer Stock*, showing just enough of his sun-kissed arms to remind just how physically big and strong he is. Or the form-fitting white sailor's trousers in *Anchors*

Aweigh that only someone in possession of some serious confidence and toned legs could pull off.

The feeling I had when I first saw Kelly remains, and can best be articulated by quoting the genius podcast *Thirst Aid Kit*: 'Who the fuck was this dancing angel and how can I dance with him?'

Kelly was an anomaly, in a way. Despite being built like a rugby player, he nonetheless started training in dance in his teens, and dropped out of law school to launch a dance studio before eventually moving into choreography and performance full time. Kelly projects an all-American brand of confident, almost brutish, masculinity that is tempered by how light he is on his feet as a dancer. When he moves, his physique becomes less intimidating; less alpha male and more pure, lithe charm. We know that this comes from years of training, endless hours of rehearsing, but it's never just that.

There are plenty of great dancers and performers, but only one Gene Kelly. His brand of charm is entirely different from that of his contemporary Fred Astaire, who was already a big star by the time Kelly broke through into motion pictures in the 1940s. Astaire, although often playing romantic leads, is entirely sexless compared to Kelly. For him, it's all about technique, and there's very little space left for us to project any sort of desire onto him. Fred Astaire dances like he'd be a selfish lover. He is aloof, his grin perfectly controlled and perfectly cold. Meanwhile, when Kelly moves, he allows us to project onto him. Underneath the tight suits and crisp shirts, there is an indescribable intensity. Call it charm, call it BDE ("Big Dick Energy", for the uninitiated). Whatever you call it, it leaves room for us to imagine.

That space for desire (whether designed by the performer, choreographer, or director—or simply ascribed by thirsty spectators) creates a line that I can draw from Kelly to Tatum.

It's different from pure lust. It's an invitation, from them to us.

III.

KELLY WAS NEVER EXPLICIT. A man of his generation starring in wholesome mid-century MGM fare, his onscreen behaviour is almost annoyingly chaste.

That's where Patrick Swayze comes in. Swayze, also a trained dancer, confidently established himself in the 1980s as a romantic leading man, an action hero and an all-round good chap. What he shares with Gene Kelly is a perfectionism that revolves around never letting us see the hard work. They perform for our enjoyment, not for us to consider their efforts.

It's impossible to not mention *Dirty Dancing*, a film that works best when seen as a metaphor for a young woman acknowledging and owning her desires. When Baby (Jennifer Grey) comes into an employee-only underground dance/sex party, she's a stand-in for all of us. Stricken at the sight of intertwined limbs, thrusting hips and sweaty torsos—she is particularly drawn to the vigorous, gravity-defying antics of Johnny (Patrick Swayze) and his dance partner Penny (Cynthia Rhodes).

When Johnny spots Baby, he tries to teach her some basic dance moves. He might as well be teaching her how to give a blowjob in the middle of a packed dance floor. He sees her watching him and tries to initiate her into pleasure (the pleasure of dancing, of course). The famous conclusion of the film, where Johnny and Baby triumphantly do the routine they've been practising is basically a public consummation of their relationship. The two of them are fucking as people cheer them on.

They know we're watching.

These films show off the male form by allowing it to move, to take up space unencumbered and unfettered—and it lets us (the audience) have the opportunity to watch them. When Kelly and Jerry dance in *Anchors Aweigh*, it's against a barren set. When Baryshnikov and Hines tap dance their way to friendship in *White Nights*, it's in an empty dance studio. The camera and our eyes follow them as they dance—angling to get closer, hungering for tighter shots on the biceps and fitted trousers.

The dance film that embraces our gaze most is undoubtedly *Magic Mike XXL*. It's a loose follow-up to Steven Soderbergh's story of a male entertainer with big dreams of owning his own business (a story loosely based on Tatum's early experiences as a go-go dancer), whose plans are thrown into disarray by the arrival of a new dancer who he takes under his wing.

Soderbergh's original film, *Magic Mike*, sets up the main characters and has a pretence of a story, but the second one dispenses with extraneous plot, embracing its finest feature: men who are there for women to look at them. The film is structured as a buddy road trip for the reunited male entertainers and Channing Tatum's character, who'd left dancing to set up his own furniture design business.

Magic Mike XXL is a series of set pieces designed to show-case the attributes and dancing abilities of its protagonists. Forgoing any real narrative logic, it lets characters find them-selves by locating their special appeal to women as strippers: the sweetness of Andre, the imposing girth of Tarzan, the sensitivity of Ken or the warm spotlight that is Mike's atten-tion. They are defined and fulfilled by fulfilling the desire of the women who watch them. Upon release, the film was quickly interpreted as a feminist masterpiece in its own right because of its freewheeling and liberal display of women of all types, shapes and temperaments gloriously lusting after the male protagonists. When they were dancing, the camera presented the goofy meathead as a generous Adonis, existing only for the pleasure of his female audience.

Dancing is foreplay. Dancing implies sex. The way these men move is creating an image of how they'll move with you, for you, on you. The way they look at their dancing partner is the way you imagine them looking at you (don't even get me started on the Gene Kelly/Cyd Charisse eye-fucking in *Singin' in the Rain*). The pleasure of watching these men dance on screen is to imagine that movement and passion applied to something else.

Dance is also a substitute for words.

It becomes an acceptable and artistic (nay, cinematic) way of utilising and presenting the male form. In films that spotlight the male dancer, the masculine body is creative rather than destructive – object rather than subject – and offers rare opportunities to its thirsty audience.

These male characters are usually not very articulate (either through language limitations or because they can't/won't articulate their feelings). 'I want to scream like he does!' yells Baryshnikov in *White Nights*. Frustrated and unable to escape his situation, as well as limited by his broken English, he furiously dances to a Russian folk song as a way of expressing his anger. Mike describes how Ginuwine's "Pony" became his signature song; it simply made him imagine all the things he'd do to a woman—and while he couldn't express that in words, he could with movement. Nobody takes Mike and his friends very seriously offstage—but onstage they are powerful and adored.

There are about 80 years between Gene Kelly and Channing Tatum. Their dancing styles are vastly different—with Kelly being an Old Hollywood performer and Tatum a self-taught former stripper—but their screen persona is the same. Their sex appeal stands on a shared principle of graceful masculinity: physically imposing, strongly built; an alpha male vibe tempered by a tender, generous dancing style full of suggestions and winks. Their dancing is a knowing invitation for us to desire them and, boy, does it work.

MEG RYAN'S NAKED AMBITIONS
Simran Hans

'TAKE THOSE OFF,' says Mark Ruffalo's Detective Malloy, gaze fixed on Meg Ryan's crotch. Her Frannie, already bare breasted, stands still. He reaches towards her and removes her underwear, camera glancing at her bottom as her knickers slide around her ankles.

Based on Susanna Moore's 1995 erotic novel set in Manhattan, Jane Campion's *In the Cut* centres on Frannie (Ryan), an English teacher who discovers a woman's severed limb outside her apartment. With the threat of sexual violence looming at the edges of her neighbourhood, Frannie finds herself involved with Malloy (Ruffalo), one of the police detectives investigating the killer at large.

The film was released in 2003, but I didn't watch it until it was broadcast on terrestrial television several years later. I was 16, in my childhood bedroom investigating, as I often did, BBC2's titillating late-night slot. The viewing experience was something of an awakening; suddenly, I understood what was meant by the term "erotic thriller".

Like most teenage girls, I hadn't yet learned how to articulate my own desire. Campion, on the other hand, seemed to have figured it out. *In the Cut* is so ripe with female desire it literally blurs at the edges as though it's vibrating at a horny, heightened frequency. When I was a teenager, female pleasure was considered a specifically feminist issue, but feminism was still a few years from permeating mainstream cultural criticism. Instead of being celebrated for the way its sex scenes inhabited a feminine perspective, the film was reviled for its shameless eroticism. Frustratingly, its cultural significance has been defined by its composite parts. Meg Ryan's composite parts.

In fact, I first heard of *In the Cut* via Judd Apatow's 2007 sex comedy *Knocked Up*. In that film, Ben (Seth Rogen), a schlubby layabout, finds himself inadvertently entangled with Katherine Heigl's attractive, careerist broadcaster Alison following a one-night stand that leaves her pregnant. What begins as an eyebrow-raising male fantasy soon morphs into a nightmare scenario for all genders and a moralistic finger jab in the direction of those who choose to indulge in casual sex. Ben doesn't have a job exactly, but is starting "an internet website" with his roommate; its purpose is to timestamp and catalogue the nude scenes of famous actresses.

> *Ben:* Say you love Meg Ryan.
> *Alison:* I do.
> *Ben:* Great. Who doesn't? Let's say you like her so much, you want to know every movie where she shows her tits. Come to our web page, exclusively, type in "Meg Ryan". Bam! *In the Cut,*

> thirty-eight minutes in, forty-eight minutes in, like an hour and ten minutes in. She's like naked that whole fuckin' movie. She does full frontal in that movie.

'I think you have to take your hat off to her in *In the Cut*, and not just because she takes her knickers off, but because she removes all traces of her celebrity,' said Andrew Anthony in a 2003 profile of Ryan for *The Observer*. There's a sleazy, facetious edge to his comment, but Anthony wasn't wrong that the role of Frannie represented a rejection of Ryan's star persona.

Ryan wasn't thought of as a character actor but instead a bonafide Movie Star™ whose brand was wholesomeness personified. She was, and still is, best known for starring in Nora Ephron's romantic comedies *When Harry Met Sally* (1989), *Sleepless in Seattle* (1993) and *You've Got Mail* (1998). I knew her for this holy trifecta too. Audiences liked that she was blond, bubbly, cutely neurotic and completely clothed— she was sexy, sure, but like most romantic comedy heroines not exactly sexual.

Consider the "I'll have what she's having" scene in *When Harry Met Sally* that cemented her as a household name. In it, Ryan's Sally sits across from Billy Crystal's Harry in a crowded New York City diner, adamant that most women fake their orgasms. When he protests, maintaining he can tell the difference, she performs one with convincing theatricality (afterwards, an onlooker tells the waiter she'll have what Sally's having). The scene is played for comedy, distancing the character (and therefore Ryan) from anything resembling an actual erotic experience. Indeed, film seems more comfortable showing Sally pretending to have a sex life than depicting her enjoying one.

In *Sleepless in Seattle* and *You've Got Mail*, Ryan's characters are barely afforded so much as a chaste kiss. Women's sexual satisfaction is not built into the romcom genre; in fact, the very acknowledgement of female carnality disrupts it. According to convention, at the end of the movie the heroine gets her "happily ever after". The acquisition of a relationship is the end goal, the prize to be won. What she does with her winnings is not of anyone's concern. A more desirous woman, on the other hand, might discover that sex (her own "happy ending", if you will) can be reward enough.

With *In the Cut*, Ryan broke free from the binds of the romcom, stepping into an actively desirous and adult role. For once, she plays a character whose pleasure is prioritised. We see this in the film's key love scene, which begins with Malloy asking Frannie to explain what happened when she was attacked earlier in the day. She begins to speak. 'Show me,' he says, standing behind her and hooking his arm around her neck. 'Left arm, or right arm?' he asks, switching position. Though both are fully clothed, there's already an erotic charge—an electrical spark of danger hangs in the air. Frannie anticipates what will happen next. 'Alright,' she says, verbalising her consent. Campion chooses to show Malloy removing his gun and placing it on Frannie's dresser, in full view. He is dropping his defences.

Frannie produces the condom, an empowered act that emphasises her agency in this particular sexual situation. She appears blurry at the edges, but Malloy remains in focus, already in her bed. As the drama moves along within the scene, Campion continually reinforces Frannie's active participation in it. The scene is not shot or blocked like an ordinary Hollywood sex scene. The camera's lens looks as though it's smeared with Vaseline, the image in soft focus: the opposite of pornography. 'Take those off,' insists Malloy, eyes gesturing towards Frannie's underwear. 'No,' she replies. He reaches over to remove them anyway. The camera doesn't linger on Ryan's bottom; instead, it hovers at waist height, travelling to the floor along with her underwear.

In her article "Meg Gets Naked", academic Lucy Bolton writes that Ryan's nudity is 'not about pin-up beauty' but rather 'represents a literal stripping bare of inhibition, enhanced by the concomitant effacement of Ryan's star persona which is affected by her physicality in the film.' When Frannie drops her defences with Malloy, her clothes are shed too.

Frannie lies on the bed, face down, as Malloy rearranges himself so that he can perform cunnilingus on her. The camera doesn't adopt Malloy's perspective, or Frannie's. Instead, Campion aims for something less voyeuristic and more sensual. It lands on the body parts that Malloy's gaze lands on, as though each area is hot to the touch after being looked at. The focus is on his fingers as they stroke the curve of her spine, and the hands that clasp hers as he enters her; the scene feels as concerned with intimacy as it does with sex. The swelling, romantic score begins to overpower the diegetic, orgasmic breathing—as if to give the couple a veneer of privacy. We see her body in motion but the camera stays focused on her face; a single cut telegraphs duration with an angle that remains the same. Frannie arches her back, her shoulders contorting with pleasure as the music crescendos and she climaxes. If Malloy got off, we don't see it—Campion is not interested. Malloy kisses the soles of her feet before the scene continues and eventually fades, its rhythm repeating like multiple orgasms.

Cinematographer Dion Beebe shoots in greenish reds and browns, leaving parts of the image hazy and out of focus; untrustworthy, like Frannie's desires. Frannie is hungry with desire but aware of the threat that letting down her guard may present. In an article titled "Sex and Self-Danger" in *Sight & Sound*, Graham Fuller describes the film as 'masochistic' in the Freudian sense, suggesting that its interest in violence against women is inherently feminine. 'The film spends plentiful time in the macho company of Malloy (Mark Ruffalo) and his wife-beating partner Rodriguez (Nick Damici),' he writes. 'It offers an extreme close-up of a woman's head bobbing over a man's loins... Strippers gyrate with grotesque lewdness.' If erotic thrillers are to be understood as paranoid responses to overt female sexuality, this reading of the film as masochistic makes sense. The rules are similar in most traditional horror films: horny women die first. Fuller stresses the film's theme of 'wilful female self-endangerment and self-entrapment.' Yet Campion gently treads the line between Frannie's attraction to the idea of danger as part of an erotic fantasy and the threat of danger itself. Importantly, Bolton notes, Campion changed the novel's ending when writing the screenplay to ensure Frannie's survival and a more redemptive conclusion that suggests 'the possibility of a future in contrast with the nihilism of the novel.'

'I can be whatever you want me to be, no problem. The only thing I won't do is beat you up,' says Malloy, meaning it.

Upon its original release, many male critics and commentators did not connect with the film or Ryan's performance in it. In *Sight & Sound*, Fuller reads *In the Cut's* 'narrow, often dimly lit interiors' as 'redolent of the film's anguished gynocentrism.'

Andrew Anthony saw the part of Frannie as 'a kind of midlife crisis', referring both to the role itself and Ryan's decision to take it. During the film's promotional tour, Ryan participated in a now-infamous interview with British TV personality Michael Parkinson—so infamous, in fact, that it would become the film's lasting legacy. 'It's awkward,' she said of being in the spotlight. 'It's not something that comes easily or sits naturally. I mean, I do it, you know, it's fine, but it doesn't seem, you know, like an easy fit.' Watching the clip back, it's shocking to think that Ryan was the one who came off badly. Parkinson is belligerent and condescending, asking terse, closed questions; it's no wonder Ryan is defensive and visibly uncomfortable.

To understand the film's feminine perspective as anguished rather than empowered – or to see its nudity as titillation – seems like a wilful misreading. The aforementioned critics don't seem to have understood the film—who it's for or what it's doing, and certainly not the urges it's led by. This wilful misreading had real-life consequences for Ryan. *In the Cut,* and the press surrounding it, kneecapped her career. Her biggest subsequent role was in Diane English's 2008 remake of George Cukor's *The Women* (a moderate box office success, but a critical flop). Over a decade later, her career has yet to bounce back.

Given that the romcom wave crested in the 1990s, Ryan's closest comparison is surely Julia Roberts. With their mile-wide smiles and similarly beguiling portfolios (Roberts starred in *Pretty Woman, My Best Friend's Wedding* and *Notting Hill*), both occupied a similar space in Hollywood. The two women are also close in age, with Ryan just six years Roberts' senior. But Roberts, unlike Ryan, has continued to work solidly throughout her career. In the years since her Academy Award win for *Erin Brockovich* in 2001, Roberts has ping-ponged between prestige dramas (*Mona Lisa Smile, Closer, Ben is Back*), family films (*Charlotte's Web, Mirror Mirror, Wonder*) and lighter romcoms (*Eat Pray Love, Mother's Day*). Her filmography contains no title as brazenly sexual as *In the Cut*. As a result, her standing as an American Sweetheart remains safe.

The next generation of Hollywood golden girls seems to be wise to the trap of being pigeonholed as an American Sweetheart like Ryan was, building more challenging fare (and casual nudity) into their filmographies from the start. Kristen Stewart, Jennifer Lawrence and Emma Stone have been canny to corner the teen market early on (*Twilight, The Hunger Games* and *Easy A*, respectively) whilst at the same time routinely picking more provocative roles (think Lawrence in *Red Sparrow*, Stone in *The Favourite* and Stewart in almost everything she's done post-*Twilight*). Not all of these individual parts have as much sexual agency as Ryan's Frannie. Lawrence's Russian ballerina-turned spy in *Red Sparrow*, for example, is at the mercy of several punishing rape scenes and, perhaps inevitably, the three actresses have been dogged by their own extracurricular scandals. Yet in playing a variety of roles as they establish their careers (as opposed to afterwards), Ryan's successors have managed to avoid being punished by the media on the basis of their projects – or their nakedness – alone.

In a 2019 interview with *The New York Times*, Ryan addressed the problem of her celebrity image, explaining that the America's Sweetheart moniker 'doesn't allow for the full expression of a person.' In Ryan's case, it didn't map neatly onto the specific creation that is Frannie; in Campion's film, her persona is swallowed whole. Elements of the character's desire remain opaque, but Ryan becomes transparent, disappearing into the role.

'But that's what movie stardom is,' Ryan told *The New York Times*. 'There's a blankness required.' Maybe to fulfil someone else's fantasy, you have to conceal certain parts of yourself. When it comes to women, both in the movies and in the bedroom, it's far easier for men to project onto a blank slate. Ryan was rejected because she wasn't considered "blank" enough as a star to pull off that role.

Perhaps it was Ryan who rejected her own star persona, relishing a part that refused to allow audiences to project their fantasies onto her. *In the Cut* holds up as a weird, anxious and genuinely sexy movie—but no good deed goes unpunished. That it was rejected only makes me want to cling to it and celebrate its "too-much" taboo all the more. The same is true of Ryan. The knowledge that one of her best and bravest performances was widely dismissed makes her onscreen vulnerability all the more potent.

I PRETENDED TO LIKE BOYS BECAUSE OF 'HIGH SCHOOL MUSICAL'

Megan Christopher

AUGUST 17TH 2007. I am 12 years old and, having just finished my first tumultuous year of high school, what's left of the summer stretches endlessly ahead. Suddenly, my phone pings.

do u wana cum watch hsm2 2nite???

This is the text that changes my life as I know it. Not four hours later, I am surrounded by a gaggle of excitable preteen girls. I stare into my popcorn as they discuss their respective summers—sleepovers, make-up, pop music, boys.

Boys.

I am – have always been – an observer of my gender's desire. At the tender age of 12, I have no way to understand that my own obsession with Anne Hathaway in *The Princess Diaries* is the same longing that the other girls feel for Zac

Efron. I feel broken; incomplete; alone. I wonder if I'm simply not trying hard enough, that if I really try then the feelings would appear eventually; that if I kiss boys then one day it'll click. I want to join in so badly that I invent this desire, mimicking the actions of my peers as they explore their own relationships with sex and attraction and love.

'I really fancy Ryan.'

I've said it before I even know what I'm saying. The words feel cold and lifeless in my mouth; a poor imitation of what I think I should say. The room goes silent for a moment, and I slowly realise that I've done something wrong.

For those unaware of the joys of the *High School Musical* franchise, Ryan Evans is one of the most heavily gay-coded characters of all time. Even the actor who plays him (Lucas Grabeel) and director (Kenny Ortega) wanted to make Ryan canonically gay but Disney refused, believing this to be inappropriate for a kids' film. Had Disney decided otherwise, I might actually have understood the concept of homosexuality on that fine summer day in 2007.

Instead, I accidentally told everyone that I fancied the gay dude – a character that no straight 12-year-old girl would ever bat an eyelid at – in a film where Zac Efron established his vice-like hold on 90 percent of the prepubescent female population.

Although funny at first (the fact that Ryan Evans was my first crush now has pride of place on my Tinder profile, and many a girl has found this little anecdote to be hilarious) there is also a sad realisation to be drawn from this story. For many young lesbians, expressing sexual attraction can be near impossible when there is no established gaze to follow.

Rather than exploring the beginnings of our sexual desire towards women, we are expected to scream at boybands and long for the embrace of a teenage heartthrob.

At the delicate point of hormonal adolescence, young people naturally find themselves searching for answers on the screen. The problem? The screen reflects a harmful binary, a concept which completely negates the existence of queer sexuality and establishes two strict perspectives—the cisgender heterosexual male and the cisgender heterosexual female.

Human sexuality does not exist within a media vacuum. In the absence of a perspective to which they might relate, young queer women often must sacrifice either their gender (by aligning themselves with the male gaze), or their desire (by succumbing to the pressure of compulsory heterosexuality). Whilst heterosexual women find their sexual awakenings through chick flicks and romance novels, lesbian sexuality is restricted to the realm of the "other", discovered only through pornography designed exclusively to cater to straight men.

Much has been written about the impact of the male gaze on lesbian consciousness, but the effect of the heterosexual female gaze is often overlooked. Although this gaze is something that feminists strive to amplify (and rightly so), the isolation that such a heteronormative movement causes for queer women must be examined.

In striving to be a "real girl" and achieve desire for the likes of Zac Efron (as my peers did), I suppressed my own sexuality for years—wrestling with the reality of my thoughts to the extent that I longed to be normal; to feel something for men other than mild irritation. My own sexual desire, the rush which I felt when I looked at a woman's breasts, or her legs, or the curve of her hip, all of this natural and beautiful energy was instantly dismissed as nothingness in favour of a fantasy I could never live up to.

Except for friendship-related joy, I feel nothing when I look at men. To my 12-year-old eyes, the floppy hair, cheeky smile and athletic physique of Zac Efron were entirely indistinguishable from that of any other man. At that age, my lack of attraction felt like an aching absence – a sign that I was not normal – provoking fears that I wasn't really a teenage girl. Instead of recognising and nurturing my own desires, I became obsessed with replicating the desires of others, channelling the giggles and the whispers and the secrets. I flipped my hair over my shoulder when boys spoke to me, lied about crushes on the lads I only felt friendship for, learned the words to say and the movements to make. All the while, I watched Nicole Kidman movies obsessively, writing off my desire as admiration and never daring to admit the number of times I'd rewatched *Moulin Rouge*. I crushed on various female teachers, blushing when they spoke to me, each time putting my feelings down to my shyness. I fell in love with my best friend, hating myself every time I wanted to be closer to her. Everything associated with desire became painful and forced and toxic. It's a difficulty that still exists for me today.

Compulsory heterosexuality, fuelled by media obsessed with straight desire, has burned into my mind a lifelong paranoia that insists my relationships are wrong and that I can never live a conventional life. Though I feign confidence in my sexuality, this doubt has never faded. Rather than finding common ground in love and sex, I intrinsically view heterosexual love as a foreign concept, out of reach for so long, a benchmark I can never quite achieve. Every interaction with men leads to a desperate examination of my own emotions before the inevitable conclusion: I cannot feel what the world wants me to feel.

High School Musical did not directly initiate my trauma, yet the influence of this film on the average teenage girl cannot be understated. The brand was everywhere, seeping from the screen into everyday life via conversations, products and spinoffs. At its heart, the *High School Musical* story worked because of its direct relation to the lives of these girls; as high schoolers ourselves, the characters and relationships on the screen became idolised, their perfect lives and oversimplified problems ideal fodder for the hormonal adolescent imagination. Troy Bolton was the dream boy, and Gabriella Montez was the sweet, innocent girl with whom we were meant to identify. And therein lies the problem: although not every girl can identify with this desire, the nature of the *High School Musical* phenomenon (and other similar teen films) characterised the teenage girl's longing for the male heartthrob as the absolute norm. Whether through Gabriella and Sharpay's attraction to Troy, Chad's relationship with Taylor, or the incredibly forced pairing of Kelsi and Ryan (gotta pair off the gays!), there was no room for homosexuality in this fictional world we were so strongly encouraged to aspire to.

Though I am no longer that terrified teenage girl, I can never get those years back. The young gay women of today face a very different, though still imperfect, state of media representation; whereas lesbians were entirely absent from my adolescence, gay teenagers can now find glimpses of their world, albeit on a smaller screen. Although mainstream teen films still avoid lesbianism, television and video games have provided new spaces for these characters to blossom. From the trendy teen series *Riverdale* and *Chilling Adventures of Sabrina* to cartoons *Steven Universe* and *The Legend of Korra*, queer girls on television are proudly showcasing their attractions for all to see—and though these representations are not without criticism, they may provide comfort for many in the same situation as I was. For girls who love video games, the gentle kisses between Ellie and Riley in *The Last of Us*, or the soft butch lesbianism of Tracer in *Overwatch* may be a comfort blanket for those discovering their own sexuality. These characters would have been cherished during my own upbringing, and I hope and trust that the future of the LGBTQ+ community is an easier one thanks to their presence.

When I was growing up, there was no character such as Tracer gracing the posters on the walls of my bedroom. There was no one to reassure me that I was not alone in wanting to kiss girls. There was no Korra and Asami to show me that I could be happy without a man in my life. There was no Ruby and Sapphire to illustrate how lesbianism could make my life complete. There was no *Riverdale, Sabrina* or *The 100* to slot my attraction to women neatly into my everyday teenage experience. So on the day that I first watched *High School Musical 2*, I sat in the living room of a girl I barely knew and desperately racked my brain for a way to prevent the group from finding out that I was not like them. That as far as I knew (and feared), I would never be like them. As they talked about how dreamy Troy was, I wondered what made him more attractive than any other boy. And as they fantasise about kissing him, I pushed thoughts of Kelsi Nielsen from my mind and declared: 'I really fancy Ryan.'

The laughter still hurts, but at least now it gets me Tinder dates.

BEAUTIFUL BOYS
Catherine Bray

PART ONE: CATCHING THE EYE

She glides into the party, oblivious to the way her clothes highlight every slight movement of her body to her advantage.

Lounging by the river in denim cut-offs and an old plaid shirt, she seems totally unaware of the fact that she is one of the most attractive girls in the world.

Sitting shyly behind the desk, her glasses perched on her nose, she has no idea how beautiful she is.

IN SCREENPLAYS AND FICTION, female-identified characters are more often than not described as some variation on "desirable" or "beautiful", and are usually unaware of that fact. In *Ways of Seeing*, John Berger posits, intelligently, that women commonly practise a splitting of the identity into two parts: herself (the surveyor) and an image of herself (the surveyed) which she must constantly scrutinise: 'From earliest childhood, she has been taught and persuaded to survey herself constantly.' This is because the way that a woman is treated in a patriarchal society is dictated first and foremost by how she looks.

That being the case, male directors frequently seem to assume that exceptionally beautiful women exist in a state of blissfully ignorant innocence about their appearance. This is pure fiction. Women in real life scrutinise and author their own appearance (a process often charged with an eroticism of its own, since it involves an estimation of desire), making every woman an auteur of a kind.

But how to credit the auteur (women) when the culturally accepted read of their accepted practice (beauty) is to pretend that we are gazing upon nature and not art? The result of this cultural convention is that the art of appearing beautiful (in the judgement of the conventional male gaze) is under-valued because in order to practise that art to perfection, a pretence is required, a pretence that the artist is innocent of the fact that they might even be practising an art. Perhaps this is one reason that many women have trouble accepting compliments. A compliment is designed to reward effort, and to acknowledge effort is to undermine the attempt at effortlessness.

How fortunate, then, to identify as male and not feel obliged to perform aesthetically on such reductive terms— where to succeed is to simultaneously forego credit, and where the simple act of acknowledging or claiming credit would undermine the very terms on which the appreciation is predicated.

Yet there is liberation in creating and performing the self—or there can be. Do male characters in fiction, and those who identify as male in real life, miss out on an opportunity to creatively perform beauty even as they escape the trap of being reduced purely to an aesthetic? And what, if anything, do we as viewers miss out on if we refuse to appreciate male beauty on the same terms as female beauty? An appreciation of beauty doesn't inherently have to be reductive—and with simple inversions of common stereotypes can even function as subversive.

PART TWO: BEAUTIFUL BOYS

He glides into the party, oblivious to the way his clothes highlight every slight movement of his body to his advantage.

Lounging by the river in denim cut-offs and an old plaid shirt, he seems totally unaware of the fact that he is one of the most attractive boys in the world.

Sitting shyly behind the desk, his glasses perched on his nose, he has no idea how beautiful he is.

HOW BEAUTY IS DEFINED is subjective, but a reluctance to appreciate beauty in a man often stems from a fear of the consequences of treating and seeing men like women. There's unease around the possibility that what has traditionally defined "man" and "woman" might be up for debate. Men are seen as the artist, not the muse; the subject, not the object. A real man is in charge of how he moves through the world, operating with agency and awareness. The passivity and innocence inherent in the "beautiful but unaware of it" trope are, according to gendered stereotypes, unmanly. A heterosexual man might be handsome, a love rat, or a rogue—but he will be aware of the power this implies. He will be characterised as an operator, a lady-killer; an active verb.

As far as art is concerned, this reluctance to appreciate passive male muses is a failure of the modern imagination. The ambiguous visual pleasure of gawking at a young man's apparently natural beauty as if he were as artless (and disposable and malleable and beautiful-without-knowing-it) as a young woman is an established tradition in Western art history.

Check out classical thirst traps like the kouroi of Ancient Greece, whole armies' worth of Renaissance sculptures, Florentine paintings such as Alessandro Allori's "Portrait of a Young Man", or any one of hundreds of other examples that take unashamed pleasure in celebrating the spare, lightly muscled androgyny of post-adolescent boys seemingly unaware of their beauty.

Look at Battistello's "Sleeping Cupid". The vulnerability of his exposed throat; the delicate cheekbones; the smooth marble of his skin; the graceful curve of his bony hips; the waves of dark hair contrasting his lily-white complexion. All attributes more often displayed in glossy photoshoots featuring women. Photoshoots depicting men normally prefer to emphasise their power, charisma, sense of humour or wisdom.

PART THREE: INNOCENCE AND EXPERIENCE

THERE HAVE ALWAYS BEEN delectable exceptions to the modern squeamishness around appreciating the male form. These allow us access to a more vulnerable male aesthetic and the possibility of a masculine ingénue.

In Hollywood, some of the most notable exceptions have included James Dean, River Phoenix, a young Johnny Depp, a young Brad Pitt, a young Leonardo DiCaprio, a young Jude Law, Robert Pattinson ten years ago—essentially anybody captured as a rising star by photographer Greg Gorman.

The overwhelming whiteness of these ingénues is disappointing but not surprising when we consider the racist refusal of Western culture to allow people of colour to ever be fully innocent. When people of colour are lauded as sexual icons in the white media, they are rarely permitted a projection of unselfconscious sexual innocence.

Perhaps the relationship of Western art to Hollywood's beautiful boys shares some of the blame for this exclusion. There is visual continuity between a "Sleeping Cupid" or "Portrait of Young Man" and the way that someone such as James Dean is described by author Michael Ferguson: 'There he is, his flaming hair at perfection, his soulful eyes, high cheekbones and mournful face classically framed [but] it was his sensitivity, his access to all his emotions that made him a new kind of teen idol and movie star.'

Note the cheekbones and access to emotion. It's not how anybody described a "man's man" such as Steve McQueen, born one year earlier than James Dean—yet if you compare pictures of the two they're not exactly hailing from an entirely different planet in terms of looks. It is the public brands of their stardom (and subsequent legacies) that differ.

Equally, the way *Vanity Fair* described River Phoenix could easily be a critique of a Renaissance portrait: 'That face: the high, broad forehead, almond-shaped eyes, the prematurely crinkled brow, full lips and retroussé nose... He was a raw, emotional open wound all the time.' The premature deaths of both Dean and Phoenix are also undoubtedly a factor in the way they are described. They're often conflated with a kind of temporary physical perfection and a sense of psychological vulnerability.

Then there's *Time* magazine on Leonardo DiCaprio (in *Total Eclipse*): a 'teen-poet sensation... the clearest image of the awful power the young, gorgeous and deranged have over those brave and stupid enough to fall in love with them.' It may be difficult to recall – given that DiCaprio's current cultural narrative is that of an unassailable established A-lister who only dates women twenty years his junior – the fervour and timbre of Leomania at its height, a time when his feline face was absolutely everywhere. Unlike Dean and Phoenix, he did not meet with real-life tragedy but died many times on screen—often in a manner befitting a true Byronic hero (drowned; shot; death from suicide).

Youthfulness is vital here because as with traditional female muses, we are talking about a kind of beauty that employs the illusion of artlessness and innocence. The attractions of older men or women are, on the whole, less likely to depend on this pretence of innocence. When discussing the beauty of that rare set of women thought to be as attractive over the age of fifty as they were when they were younger (Charlotte Rampling, say, or Isabelle Huppert), writers talk about their sexual authority; their power; their knowing quality. There's the promise of expertise. Men are typically ascribed these things from a much younger age; they are expected to embody authority and experience, even when they have precisely zero of either. Innocence and a lack of self-awareness in older people is rarely a sign of attractiveness and can be a sign of decline, a failure to have matured. "A second childhood" is not a compliment.

PART FOUR: TIMOTHÉE

2018 SAW TIMOTHÉE CHALAMET installed as the current poster boy for vulnerable lily-white male beauty. At 22, he became the youngest Best Actor Academy Award nominee in eighty years. He was nominated for his precocious, faun-like turn in Luca Guadagnino's *Call Me by Your Name*, a simultaneously erotic and hazily under-sexed adaptation of André Aciman's overripe peach of a novel. It's a performance that perfectly simulates the appeal of a young person completely unaware of their own power.

That year, he also costarred in vivacious coming-of-age portrait *Lady Bird*. Writer-director Greta Gerwig received only the fifth Academy nomination for Best Director to go to a female director. 2019 saw the UK release of *Beautiful Boy*, an unconvincing flail of a film, despite all the usually excellent talents involved. Chalamet, as a meth-addicted teenager, manages to be one of the better things about it. He is more or less convincing in scenes depicting the crafty faux-casual pretence of the addict, pretending he doesn't really mind where that next hit is coming from.

Taken together, *Call Me by Your Name*, *Lady Bird* and *Beautiful Boy* make up a kind of variably successful hat-trick of progressiveness, and fair play to Chalamet and his management for those choices. In little more than a year, he became an LGBTQ+ icon, a friend to the feminist cause and spokesperson for the mental illness that is addiction. He also announced he would donate his salary from forthcoming Woody Allen film *A Rainy Day in New York* to charity in the wake of renewed allegations against the director. What had you done before your twenty-third birthday?

The physical descriptors of Chalamet are strikingly similar to those which greeted the "R-Pattz" phenomenon (*Vanity Fair* on Robert Pattinson: 'An exquisite beauty—with perfectly formed red, red lips and a face that might have been dreamed by the Romantic poets').

But Chalamania embodies the next iteration. Whereas Pattinson looked uneasy in the spotlight, had no official social media accounts, and was described by director Josh Safdie as being 'like a pop martyr, in a weird way,' Chalamet is a beautiful boy for the Instagram era. None of the many cultural critiques and appreciations of Chalamet is as absolutely fitting as the Instagram account which photoshops him into Renaissance art. If it didn't exist, you'd have to make it up.

So how are we to square a social media presence with the innocence of an ingénue who has no idea what effect they are having on people? Social media is predicated on the audience, and on the subject knowingly turning themselves into an object for people to scrutinise. Is it possible to maintain an illusion that you don't have any idea how beautiful you are when you have millions of followers telling you exactly that?

Physically, Chalamet fits the template of post-war Hollywood's beautiful boys: the floppy hair, the languid eyes, the skinniness (there has yet to be a plus-size lad lauded in quite this vein). He has the sensitivity and the vulnerability down, too. The key difference between Chalamet and past iterations is that he is presented as more or less enjoying it all, and this marks an important turning point. As *i-D* describes him in a feature (in which he was interviewed by the music industry's own Timothée Chalamet equivalent, Harry Styles), he is 'sensitive, honest, thoughtful, polite, goofy and self-aware. He's in touch with his feminine side and he smiles. A lot.'

Presumably, there are days when Chalamet loathes his fandom—intense scrutiny is tiresome and only a psychopath would enjoy it 24/7. Unlike Robert Pattinson, who was obviously unwilling to play the naïf who just can't quite believe his good fortune, whoever manages the content on the Chalamet social media accounts has (at the time of writing) the good sense never to let any exasperation show. In a medium where the projection of innocent obliviousness isn't credible, another route must be sought: the illusion that you can't believe your luck and are enjoying every moment of the ride.

If innocence is not possible, then what supplants it is knowingness. Knowingness leaves room for a subversive delight in your own desirability. It is in this subversion (much more than in what they choose to wear) that some modern men present an alternative form of masculinity; they allow their image to be gazed upon and consumed in a way that women have traditionally experienced. Because social media is a conscious documentation of the self, heterosexual men are no longer denied the opportunity to luxuriate in the pleasures of being looked at, no longer excluded from the erotic possibilities of self-construction (drag queens, of course, have always enjoyed this right, but have historically paid a high price for it in conservative societies).

For women, social media helps destroy the tendency to deny active participation in the construction of one's own image, freeing women to accept credit for the aesthetic labour they undertake (hashtags such as #wokeuplikethis or #makeupfree are often used in retrograde ways because they deny this agency). Instead of being expected to deny all complicity in the construction of their own image, women are increasingly able to acknowledge their authorship and authority. Authority is a necessary precondition of power. Boys and girls finally become both muse and auteur. Subject and object. The thing that we desire, and the author of that desire.

TEENAGE GIRLS KNOW SOMETHING WE DON'T
Sheila O'Malley

THE "NEW KID" ON THE TV series *Eight is Enough* had dark hair that was feathered and parted in the middle. His face was beautiful: big brown eyes, long eyelashes, a sensitive mouth. He had serious presence. The character's name was Jeremy Andretti and he was played by Ralph Macchio. *Eight is Enough* had run for years as an ensemble show, and Macchio was a late addition, probably as catnip to attract a younger audience. I was too young to watch the show in its first season but started tuning in with religious fervour once Jeremy arrived. I gravitated towards him like a moth to the flame. I couldn't put into words what I felt. Jeremy was tough but sensitive. He was sulky but emotional. He harboured a secret love for Fred Astaire and Ginger Rogers movies. If you could create "The Perfect Fantasy Object for Sensitive Tweens" in a lab, Jeremy Andretti would be it. I had no way of knowing my passion for him was not unique—that across the nation thousands of young fans like me were having the same reaction to the new dark-haired boy. I felt like he was my own personal discovery.

Three years later, after a heartbreaking performance as Johnny in the 1983 ensemble film *The Outsiders*, Macchio became an enormous star all on his own with *The Karate Kid* (1984). *The Karate Kid* was such a juggernaut that almost 35 years later it's still such a common reference point that the television series spinoff *Cobra Kai* basically justifies its own existence. The weighty presence of Pat Morita both grounded Macchio and also let him soar. He was a natural star.

I was not a sophisticated and media-savvy child, but when *The Karate Kid* hit and Macchio exploded (dominating the cover of every teen magazine in the land), I was unsurprised. After all, hadn't I already perceived his awesomeness in *Eight is Enough*? I felt a sense of personal ownership of him. His nationwide fame was exciting to me—but there was sadness, too. He was no longer "my secret". Everyone knew now. But I saw him first.

Teenage girls make excellent coal mine canaries if you want to know where pop culture is headed; they sense what's coming before the rest of us. They know what the next "big thing" will be; who is going to be huge. The reasons for this are multi-layered and not easily explained. In a culture invested in policing women's natural responses, inhibiting self-expression and corralling the female sex drive like you would a wild animal—girls have a lot of steam to let off. When steam builds up, it doesn't just hiss, it shrieks like a tea kettle. The Beatles were greeted in America by a million shrieking tea kettles. The 20th century vibrates with the ear-piercing screams of teenage girls.

The moneymakers, studios, agents and directors have their ear to the ground for the crescendo of screaming girls. Screams mean money. People who were baffled by the rise of Justin Bieber (asking: 'Where the hell did he come from and when will he go back there?') had not been paying attention and did not think the screams of girls were worth listening to. And so they were taken by surprise. Nobody likes to be taken by surprise, and so they made fun of Bieber's haircut, his voice, his songs and – predictably – they sneered at the devotion he inspired. Teenage girls are accustomed to this sort of treatment. You can make fun of them all you want, but they will continue to plaster their bedroom walls with posters of David Cassidy, Leif Garrett, Lance Kerwin, or (in earlier generations) Elvis Presley, Ricky Nelson, Tab Hunter, James Dean, or (now) Justin Bieber, Robert Pattinson and Zac Efron. These figures give teenage girls the space to swoon around in sexual and romantic fantasies without shame and judgement. The smart "powers that be" know that if you tap into the teenage girl demographic you tap into loyalty that can't be bought, manufactured, or even really planned for. (Visit Graceland today and you will be surrounded by elderly women, all of whom loved Elvis when they were teenagers. Teenage girls are loyal until death, and beyond.)

"Sex appeal" wasn't invented in the 20th century, but the new art forms (movies, still photography, popular music), aided by the rise in technology which could spread the word farther and faster, changed the game. Silent-era star Rudolph Valentino brought a sensational sexuality to the screen that was both explosive and destabilising. He was beautiful, as opposed to handsome. His movements were sultry, erotic; he projected sexual pleasure without embarrassment. All of these were seen as stereotypically femme qualities, so there was a gender-bending aspect to Valentino's appeal (a commonality of male stars who inspire female devotion: they are tough and soft, simultaneously). The power of what Valentino was doing, and the newness of it, can still be felt today when you watch his films. Women flipped out.

Then, as now, female fan frenzy was treated with suspicion and displeasure. Women screaming about something will always bring concerned tut-tutting from the wings: What is this world coming to when women love XYZ? What does it say about "our world" and "where we are now" that women have decided to love this weird thing that "we" (whoever "we" are) don't approve of or understand? Predictably, the press turned on Valentino, sneering at his "femininity", the criticisms reeking of misogyny and homophobia. He wasn't seen as a "real man", and certainly not a real American man. That women chose to love him was seen as an indictment of the choices available to them in America. This is the kind of top-heavy cultural critique laid on women. They can't flip out over something without op-ed columnists across the land worrying about what it means for the country and for future generations. Women's desires – however frivolous – are seen as ominous portents for what might be wrong with society. Perhaps this is because men are assumed to belong to themselves and women are assumed to belong to everyone—and so what teenage girls decide to do is deemed everybody's business.

There may also be in it a vestige of the Victorian idea that women are childlike creatures who need to be guided towards the proper responses—responses that won't threaten the male status quo. That status quo has a vested interest in women "presenting" a certain way. Whatever the case may be, when women decide *en masse* to love Rudolph Valentino or Justin Bieber or Elvis Presley or *Twilight*, the response in some quarters can only be described as "threatened". As silly as it sounds, some men take it personally. The egotism is astounding.

In Samuel Charters' short novel *Elvis Presley Calls His Mother After the Ed Sullivan Show*, an exhausted Elvis regales his mother with stories of life on the road, the people he meets and the hostile reactions he receives from men, angry boyfriends and pissed-off parents. At one point, he meets the father of one of his fans, and the father unexpectedly opens up to Elvis, saying:

> So when you see a picture of some singer or movie star on your daughter's wall, you realize she's beginning to think about something that doesn't have anything to do with you. In the beginning, you don't think too much about it. It's just a sign that she's growing up. But when she begins to talk about the face on the wall so much, then you get jealous. You really do, Elvis, even though you realize it's a silly way to act, you can't help yourself... For every girl who jumps and screams at one of your concerts, you've got a man who's jealous, somewhere inside himself—even if he won't tell himself that's what it is. He doesn't like you at all.

This is an insightful passage, especially when you think of cultural commentators moaning, sneering and belittling whatever it is adolescent girls choose to love. Charters clocks the uneasiness that figures such as Presley inspire in male onlookers. Presley, and the sound of girls screaming about him, brings on a feeling of hopeless inadequacy in the men who don't get it, a sense of being left out. When women launch into public fantasies like this, it means they're not solely focused on the men in their lives. They have private inner worlds that men can't access. The underlying impression is that many men have a sense of frustrated ownership over women.

There were so many hand-wringing think-pieces about the popularity of Stephanie Meyers' *Twilight* series – not to mention E. L. James's *Fifty Shades* series – that you would have thought teenage girls had taken to tossing cannonballs off overpasses onto rush hour traffic, as opposed to grooving to the erotic possibilities in a book series. That girls loved *Twilight* was treated as a national emergency.

The books continue to be deconstructed by worrywarts ('This is an abusive relationship'; 'Edward is so controlling'; 'It's badly written') because the sight of girls gasping with pleasure can't simply be left alone. There's got to be more to it. A generation of GIs swooned over pin-up posters of Betty Grable and Rita Hayworth and nobody batted an eye. Nobody worried about what the world was coming to, why men had chosen to love Betty Grable and what it all meant. Nobody thought men wouldn't be able to tolerate relationships with real-life women just because they swooned over Hayworth. But women and girls storming the barricades to get to Elvis Presley, or writing libraries of *Twilight* fanfic, or crowding into Rockefeller Plaza at 3 a.m. to score a good spot for the performance from the cast of *High School Musical* on *The Today Show* generates a whirlwind of concerned commentary.

I have often wondered if critical analysts resist engaging with certain figures merely because they're being pointed out by throngs of screaming tweens. Pop culture writers want to uncover the next cool thing, but maybe they don't want to be told by a bunch of girls where to look. Thus, critics ignored a juggernaut like *High School Musical*—or at least didn't take it seriously, and certainly didn't take Zac Efron's star potential seriously. (When 2014's *Neighbors* came out, many critics expressed surprise at Efron's deep performance. Teenage girls who loved him in *High School Musical* were not surprised at all.)

Critics mocked *Twilight* incessantly and mocked Robert Pattinson and Kristen Stewart for their red carpet slouching, bad acting and overall attitudes. But who was right in the long run? Look at the fascinating careers of both Pattinson and Stewart post-*Twilight*. Both actors have devoted themselves to challenging and often non-commercial work. Those screaming teenage girls who clocked Pattinson and Stewart first, who loved them first and loved them best, now follow Pattinson and Stewart anywhere. *Twilight* fans will watch films directed by Kelly Reichardt, the Safdie brothers, Woody Allen, James Gray, David Cronenberg, Olivier Assayas, Werner Herzog and Brady Corbet. This is loyalty that goes beyond fandom. It is love, in its purest and most undistilled form.

The smart critics pay attention to the hissing of tea kettles about to explode. There will always be those who ignore the sound of girls screaming and refuse to take a deeper look at, say, Zac Efron, to see what might be there, to try to see what girls see, or to understand the appeal. It's much easier to mock, to sneer, to dismiss and, if much of it comes from jealousy (as the passage above suggests), there is still a lot of work to do.

But what would happen if critics took the tastes of teenage girls seriously? What would happen if they acknowledged that teenage girls are often weathervanes, pointing out the way the wind is blowing? Teenage girls see farther, go deeper into their fantasies, and most certainly scream louder. Maybe the next time critics hear thousands of girls screaming, they shouldn't roll their eyes in annoyance. Instead, maybe they should follow the sound.

ABOUT THE EDITOR

CHRISTINA NEWLAND is an award-winning journalist with bylines at *Sight & Sound, The Guardian, Little White Lies, VICE, Hazlitt, The Ringer* and others. She has written on a variety of subjects including culture, fashion, history and sport, but is best known as a film critic and writer with specialist knowledge of American film history. In her writing, she has shown a consistent interest in boxing and the boxing film. In addition, she writes longform biography on figures of cultural significance, from forgotten female movie producers to gypsy prizefighters during the Second World War.

In 2015, Christina was awarded the Intellect Books (Masoud Yadzani) Award for Excellence in Film Scholarship. She also contributes a monthly print column on film and fashion to *Little White Lies*. She tweets at @christinalefou and you can find her work at thebetamaxrevolt.com.

CONTRIBUTORS

SARAH ELIZABETH ADLER is a journalist based in Washington, DC. Her writing on science, art and culture topics – from the psychology of animal cuteness to the secret lives of ghostwriters – has appeared in *The Atlantic, California* magazine and elsewhere. Working primarily as a health and lifestyle reporter by day, she has a special interest in covering LGBT issues as well as book and theatre criticism. She tweets at @seadler_.

IZZY ALCOTT is a particularly nosy writer from the UK. She loves to write about the treasured secrets and buried truths that make people who they are—so don't invite her to tea because she'll be rooting through your bedside drawer the moment your back is turned. Izzy writes for various magazines and websites under a variety of pen names, under the impression that this makes her as elusive and intriguing as Holly Golightly. It almost definitely doesn't.

CORRINA ANTROBUS is a born-and-bred East Londoner, film writer, podcaster and Founder of The Bechdel Test Fest—a celebration of films that present women in a positive and dynamic light. In 2017 she was awarded a Trailblazer Award from Melissa Silverstein's *Women and Hollywood*, which advocates and agitates for gender diversity and inclusion in the global film industry. She is a regular BIFA juror and judged the Aswan's International Women Film Festival in Egypt in 2018. She is a film writer and podcaster who also meddles in film distribution, marketing and exhibition, and who loves nothing more than attending film festivals and sniffing around old cinemas around the world. She tweets at @corrinacorrina and @BechdelTestFest.

AMY V. BLAKEMORE writes about the body. Her work has been published in *The Kenyon Review, PANK, Wigleaf, The Indiana Review, Redivider* and *Paper Darts*, and she has received support from the Association of Writers and Writing Programs, WritingxWriters and the Fine Arts Work Center in Provincetown, Massachusetts. She is at work on her first novel, a horror story about girlhood, and a collection of essays on eating disorders, queerness and television. She tweets at @AmyV_Blakemore.

ANNA BOGUTSKAYA is film programmer, podcaster, creative producer and writer currently based in London. In the past, she worked at Pedro Almodóvar's El Deseo and the BFI London Film Festival, ran Shooting People and programmed for the British Film Institute. Currently, she is Head of Arts and Culture at DICE, programme advisor for several film festivals, BIFA juror, co-host on The Bigger Picture podcast and Festival Director of BAFTA-recognised Underwire Festival. In 2016, she co-founded horror film collective The Final Girls and hosts their podcast. She often writes and talks about film for several outlets, and can be found retweeting pictures of cats at @annabdemented.

CATHERINE BRAY is a commissioner, producer and writer-director whose first feature film as a producer was Charlie Lyne's '90s teen movie doc *Beyond Clueless* (2014), followed by iPlayer essay feature *Fear Itself* (2015). She is a co-founder of Loop, whose work includes *Missing Episode* for BBC2 (2017), *Fish Story* (2017), and *Lasting Marks* (2018). Her debut as writer-director is an hour-long essay film, premièring on BBC4 Christmas 2019. Catherine freelances as a print and broadcast journalist, including for the BBC, Channel Five, BFI, *The Guardian*, *Time Out* and *Variety*. She is Head of Arts at Little Dot Studios and tweets at @catherinebray.

MEGAN CHRISTOPHER is a freelance film and culture journalist based in Manchester, UK. After graduating from the University of Manchester in 2017, Megan co-founded Much Ado About Cinema, a film website dedicated to the amplification of diverse voices in criticism. From here, she has gone on to cover festivals such as Cannes, Berlinale and BFI Flare. Since leaving Much Ado in 2019 to focus on freelance work, Megan has written for outlets such as *Sight & Sound*, *Little White Lies* and *Gay Essential*, podcasted for *Screen Queens* and spoken in front of hundreds on her favourite subject: Cersei Lannister. Her writing tends to focus on issues of identity and sexuality. Outside of journalism, Megan's main interests are WKD, crop tops and lesbianism. She tweets at @tinyfilmlesbian.

CAROLINE GOLUM is a filmmaker, programmer and critic living in Brooklyn, New York (by way of Southern California). Her writing has appeared in the now-defunct (but legendary) *The L Magazine*, the still-active and priceless digest *Screen Slate*, the august pages of *Little White Lies* and *Variety Online*. Her directorial debut *A Feast of Man* premièred in 2017 at the Sidewalk Film Festival and went on to screen at film festivals across the US. When not working for The Man, she is usually at, writing about, or trying to make a movie. She tweets at @carolineavenue.

SIMRAN HANS is a culture writer and film critic for *The Observer*. You can also read her work in/on *BuzzFeed, Dazed & Confused, The FADER, The Guardian, Little White Lies, Mubi, New Statesman, Pitchfork, Reverse Shot, Sight & Sound* and *Variety,* among others. From 2015–2018, she co-programmed feminist screening series Bechdel Test Fest, for which she won a Women & Hollywood Trailblazer award. She lives in London and tweets at @heavier_things.

PAMELA HUTCHINSON is a freelance writer, critic and film historian, specialising in silent and classic cinema as well as stardom and women's film history. She contributes regularly to *Sight & Sound*, the *Guardian, Criterion* and *Indicator* and often appears on BBC radio. She is a guest tutor at the National Film and Television School and a member of the London Film Critics' Circle. Her publications include essays in several edited collections as well as a monograph on *Pandora's Box* (BFI, 2018). She is also the editor of *30-Second Cinema* (Quarto, 2019) and the founder and editor of Silent London, a silent cinema website. She tweets at @pamhutch and @silentlondon.

RAECHEL ANNE JOLIE is a writer, educator and media maker. She holds a PhD in Media Studies (with a minor on Feminist and Critical Sexuality Studies) from the University of Minnesota. Her creative nonfiction, journalism and criticism has been published in *Teen Vogue, Mask Magazine, Bitch Magazine, In These Times* and many more. Her memoir *Rust Belt Femme* is forthcoming from Belt Publishing. She is a proud cat momma, a witch and a longtime vegan. She currently resides in Minneapolis (Minnesota) and she tweets at @reblgrrlraechel.

SOPHIE MONKS KAUFMAN is a writer and creative based in London. *I Do Not Sleep,* her first film, was completed in 2017. *Close-ups: Wes Anderson*, her first book, was published by Harper Collins in 2018. 'The Original Sin of Claire Denis', her first season programmed, played at the British Film Institute in 2019. She works mainly in film journalism and is contributing editor at the world's most beautiful film magazine, *Little White Lies*. She tweets at @sopharsogood.

JESSICA KIANG is an International Critic for *Variety*, covering all the major European and Asian festivals. She also writes for *Sight & Sound*, BBC Culture and *The Playlist*, where she spent five verbose years as Features Editor. She has served on festival juries from Iceland to Romania to Egypt and most recently was a judge of the 2019 Toronto International

Film Festival Platform competition. She lives in Berlin – or at least keeps her stuff there – and is unhealthily invested in her near-perfect track record of not beeping when going through airport security. She tweets at @jessicakiang.

VIOLET LUCCA is Web Editor and Digital Director at *Harper's Magazine* and a member of the New York Critics' Circle. She regularly contributes writing to *Sight & Sound* and was formerly the Digital Producer at *Film Comment*. Her writing has appeared in *The New York Times, Sight & Sound, The Village Voice, Reverse Shot, Criterion*, and others. Lucca studied film and film production at the University of Iowa, graduating with honours, and received her Master's degree in cinema studies from New York University in 2009. She has also worked at the Byrd Hoffman Watermill Center and WNYC. She tweets at @unbuttonmyeyes.

WILLOW CATELYN MACLAY is a writer/film critic living in Canada. She is co-author of the upcoming book, *Corpses, Fools and Monsters: An Examination of Transgender Cinema*. She has written for outlets such as *The Village Voice* and RogerEbert.com. She is currently writing for MUBI and her own website, Curtsies and Hand Grenades. In addition to being a film critic she hopes to shoot a self-financed film this autumn entitled *Sugar Coma*. She tweets at @willow_catelyn.

SO MAYER is a writer and activist. Their books include *Political Animals, From Rape to Resistance* and *The Cinema of Sally Potter*. Their writing about queer and feminist film appears in *Sight & Sound, The F-Word, cléo* and *Literal,* and their essays feature in Roxane Gay's *Not That Bad: Dispatches from Rape Culture* and *At the Pond: Swimming at the Hampstead Ladies' Pond.* After a decade in academia teaching film studies and creative writing at Cambridge, Queen Mary, King's College London and others, they work as a bookseller at Burley Fisher Books and with queer feminist film curation collective Club des Femmes. So is a Co-Founder of Raising Films, a campaign and community for parents and carers in film.

SHEILA O'MALLEY is a film critic, a regular contributor to RogerEbert.com and a columnist for *Film Comment.* Her writing has also appeared in *The New York Times, The L.A. Times, The Criterion Collection, Sight & Sound, The Moviegoer* and others. She wrote the narration scripts for two Academy Awards Lifetime Achievement tribute reels: Gena Rowlands (read by Angelina Jolie), and Anne V. Coates (read by Diane Lane). She is a member of the New York Film Critics' Circle and writes a blog called *The Sheila Variations.* She tweets at @sheilakathleen.

ANNE RODEMAN is a queer writer and performer based in New York City. Her work has appeared in *Slate, Vulture, VH1* and *McSweeney's.* She has performed all over the city, most notably hosting a five-year run of her variety show, *So Into It* at The Upright Citizens Brigade Theatre. She co-hosts the actress-centric podcast *You Might Know Her From.* She tweets at @rodemanne.

ELOISE ROSS is a writer, critic, lecturer and film programmer based in Melbourne, Australia. Eloise has a PhD in cinema studies, and her research specialises in sound studies, Hollywood history and the phenomenological experience of engaging with the cinema. She also co-hosts the podcast *Cultural Capital*, and occasionally indulges in radio broadcasting to spread more love about old movies. As Co-Curator of the Melbourne Cinémathèque she continues to share that love of old movies, and definitely spends a lot of time desiring things from the film world—locations, clothing, stars. She tweets at @EloiseLoRoss.

LAUREN VEVERS is a writer, filmmaker and critic from Newcastle upon Tyne. Her plays, *Trashed* and *Bassline*, were included on the Pint-Sized Playwriting Longlist for 2018 and 2019. Her debut short film as a writer/director, *Love Spell*, has been awarded funding from BFI Network and is in production with Freya Films. She runs creative writing workshops for young people and community groups across the North. She tweets @laurenvevers.